Disciples of the Buddha

Disciples of the Buddha

edited by
Zenno Ishigami

translated by
Richard L. Gage
and
Paul McCarthy

Kosei Publishing Co. · Tokyo

The five disciples of the Buddha illustrated on
the cover are details from *Koso Zuzo* (Portraits of
Eminent Priests), a scroll executed in ink on paper
by the Buddhist priest Kan'yu in 1163 and designated
an Important Cultural Property by the Japanese govern-
ment. The figures are reproduced courtesy of Ninna-ji
temple, Kyoto. The disciples depicted are, counter-
clockwise from top right, Sariputta, Moggallana,
Maha-Kassapa, Ananda, and Subhuti.

Editorial supervision by EDS Inc., Editorial &
Design Services. Book design, typography, and cover
design by Becky Davis, EDS Inc. The text of this book
is set in a computer version of Plantin with a
computer version of Optima for display.

Copyright and translation acknowledgments
follow page 206.

First English edition, 1989
Second printing, 1990

Published by Kōsei Publishing Co.,
Kōsei Building, 2-7-1 Wada, Suginami-ku, Tokyo 166, Japan.
Copyright © 1989 by Kōsei Publishing Co.; all
rights reserved. Printed in Japan.

ISBN 4-333-01423-9
LCC Card No. applied for

CONTENTS

OTHER DISCIPLES

Map follows page 39

INTRODUCTION

The history of Buddhism begins with Shakyamuni, the historical Buddha, who lived in India over twenty-five hundred years ago. Shakyamuni propagated his teachings orally, mainly in the course of many long journeys on foot in northeastern India. The early Buddhist scriptures include many accounts of Shakyamuni addressing villagers, listening to the elderly, teaching and admonishing his disciples, and talking with adherents of other religions. He comforted disciples who were troubled in spirit or physically ill, encouraging them and seeking to awaken them to eternal truths. Sometimes he would rest in the shade of tall trees along country roads, enjoying a brief respite as he chatted with his disciples. It was through these varied contacts that more and more disciples were drawn to the Buddha and to the Sangha, the monastic community of believers.

The Buddha was a person of great tolerance and magnanimity: he did not recognize the hierarchy of castes that was so entrenched in the India of his day but admitted anyone into the Sangha, from priestly Brahman to lowly Sudra. Precedence within the Sangha depended not on birth or social status but simply on seniority. Many people who had been of low status in secular society distinguished themselves in the Sangha.

When he attracted his first five followers, the nucleus of the Sangha, the Buddha was unknown in most of India, no doubt partly because the land of his birth was a small one in the far north of the subcontinent. No matter how well known he may have been in his own country, the kingdom of the Shakyas, it was quite otherwise in such great states as Magadha and Kosala. Around that time a famous religious teacher named Sanjaya was active in Rajagaha, the capital of Magadha. He had two especially outstanding disciples, Sariputta and Moggallana. The Buddha's conversion of these two, who then persuaded the rest of Sanjaya's disciples to follow them, marked a major turning point in the development of the Sangha. Thanks to this mass conversion, the Buddha's name quickly became known throughout northeastern India.

If we wish to understand the Buddha and the age in which he lived, it is extremely helpful to study the lives of his disciples. After the Buddha's death his disciples recollected as accurately as possible their teacher's words and deeds and strove to emulate them. We must never forget that the earliest Buddhist scriptures were based on the reminiscences of these disciples, who transmitted his words and deeds as faithfully as memory permitted. It was through their teaching of the Way to enlightenment that the Sangha continued to grow.

As might be expected, there was opposition to the Buddha and his teachings. For example, the Buddha's cousin Devadatta, who tried to revive extreme ascetic practices that the Buddha had discarded, came to be regarded in later times as a rebel and a heretic. Devadatta promoted practices that bore no relation whatsoever to the ordinary life of society. There were those who agreed with him, and a split developed in the Sangha. Sariputta and Moggallana set out to persuade the misled disciples of their error and succeeded in bringing some of them back to the fold. In the end, Devadatta severed all relations with the Sangha. It is this fact that led early Buddhists to brand him a traitor to Buddhism; yet in later scriptures he is presented as the object of the Buddha's compassion and is described as finally attaining enlightenment.

Sariputta and Moggallana died when the Buddha was well advanced in years. Indeed, the Buddha's last years were filled with sorrowful events. Nevertheless, he continued to watch over his disciples with deep compassion. This is illustrated by a passage in the Anguttara-nikaya, an early scripture, that lists briefly the ways in which various disciples were preeminent. "Monks, chief among my disciples who are monks of long standing is Anna-Kondanna. Chief among those of great wisdom is Sariputta. Chief among those of supernatural powers is Great Moggallana. Chief among those who uphold minute observance of forms is Kassapa the Great." The list continues, naming forty-one monks, thirteen nuns, eleven laymen, and ten laywomen as outstanding in some quality.

Chulla-Panthaka, for example, is noted as the disciple foremost in manifesting different physical forms at will and also as foremost in liberating the mind. He, who had been regarded as a fool, is given not one but two epithets of praise. Lakuntaka-Bhaddiya is listed as foremost in beauty of voice, Sona-Kutikanna as foremost in speaking well, and Sivali as foremost in receiving alms when out begging. Still more interesting is the fact that Kunda-Dhana is described as "the first to receive food tickets." During the rainy season, when it was impossible for the monks to go out on their begging rounds, they took their meals together in the refectory; at such times Kunda-Dhana was always the first to arrive to receive the necessary food ticket.

The monk listed as foremost among "those who assign quarters" is Dabba-Mallaputta, from which we can tell that specific tasks were assigned to monks in the Sangha. The Buddha's half brother, Nanda, was unable to forget his wife even after entering the Sangha, and was therefore regarded as being particularly prone to the weaknesses of the flesh. Yet he is listed as the monk foremost among those "who guard the doors of sense." He is praised in this way because he illustrates that even a man of weak character can learn to strengthen himself and control his desires under the Buddha's guidance.

Radha is described as continually asking questions about everything. The Buddha once rebuked him for asking about things that had no connection with religious practice and pursuit of the Way. But Radha must have learned to bring his curiosity and argumentativeness under control, for he is warmly praised as foremost among "impromptu speakers." Mogharajan was foremost among "wearers of coarse robes," and the Buddha is said to have advised the other monks to model themselves on him in this regard.

The truth is that everyone has some strong point or talent that others might well emulate. This list teaches us that we should not despise ourselves but should practice diligently so that even our weaknesses may in time become strengths.

As the account in the Anguttara-nikaya shows, the Buddha gave his compassionate attention to all his disciples, without discriminating among them in any way. It is not hard to see why the disciples so loved and venerated their teacher. These brief descriptions of disciples enable us to glimpse their individual characters—humorous, or playful, or not quite up to the mark in some respect. And the nature of their teacher is thrown into clear relief as we see him discerning their characters and then providing the helpful advice each one needs. Taken together, the descriptions convey the manifold aspects of the Buddha's greatness.

When we speak of the Buddha's disciples, we usually mean the so-called ten great disciples. Yet the Buddha himself treated all his disciples equally; he himself never used the expression "the ten great disciples." That term derives from a later age, when Buddhists selected the ten who seemed most eminent to them. In fact there are several lists of ten, though the following disciples are most often included: Sariputta, Moggallana, Maha-Kassapa, Upali, Ananda, Anuruddha, Rahula, Kacchayana, Subhuti, and Punna-Mantaniputta. But it is important to realize that there are other groupings of eminent disciples, as well. There are the sixteen *arahants* who are said to have vowed to one another that they would faithfully transmit the Buddha's teachings, and the five hundred *arahants* who assembled immediately after the Buddha's death to compile the Buddhist canon. All these disciples have been revered through the centuries in Buddhist lands.

This book presents the stories of twenty-eight disciples: the above-mentioned ten great disciples and eighteen other disciples, both ordained and lay. Readers will find that not all the Buddha's disciples were "model students" from the start. Some gave in to sloth in the course of their religious practice and began to fall away, only to be reawakened by the admonitions of the Buddha and more advanced disciples. Others reached a spiritual impasse at a certain stage of their practice and had to endure great mental suffering to attain enlightenment. Still others found themselves unable to sever their attachments to the world even after entering the Sangha; some joined the Sangha and left it several times before finally attaining enlightenment. Sharing the experiences of these disciples not only teaches us about their varied approaches to religious practice but also helps us understand the warm relationship they enjoyed with the Buddha.

The tales in this book are adapted from accounts of disciples recorded in the original Pali texts or Chinese translations of a variety of early scriptures. The sources include the Agama sutras; the Nikayas, including the above-mentioned Anguttara-nikaya; the Vinaya-pitaka; the *Theragatha* (Verses of the Elder Monks) and the *Therigatha* (Verses of the Elder Nuns), together with their commentaries; the *Dhammapada* (Verses on the Law) and its commentary, the *Dhammapada-atthakatha;* and the Avadana literature. Because the book is intended for easy reading rather than scholarly scrutiny, I have not specified what portions of each story are taken from which text. I have also taken the liberty of slightly adapting passages quoted from the scriptures.

Most personal and place names are transliterated

from Pali, the language of the earliest scriptures, but a few names and terms that are best known in their Sanskrit forms are transliterated from that language instead. Interested readers will find the orthodox Pali and Sanskrit transliterations of major names and terms in the glossary.

Zenno Ishigami
PROFESSOR OF BUDDHIST STUDIES
TAISHO UNIVERSITY, TOKYO

THE TEN GREAT DISCIPLES

SARIPUTTA
Foremost in Wisdom

Both politically and philosophically India was in turmoil at the time that Prince Siddhattha of the
Shakyas, later to be known as the Buddha Shakyamuni, abandoned secular life in search of enlightenment. New political states were constantly coming
into being; at one time as many as sixteen were engaged in struggle.

Many people were coming to feel that the estab-
lished Brahman teachings could not lead to spiritual
liberation. Consequently, advocates of various new
doctrines emerged, and increasing numbers of people
awaited the appearance of a teacher who would guide
them to true spiritual deliverance. Many strove to become such teachers themselves.

Philosophers and men of religion with these aims
tended to gravitate toward Rajagaha, the capital of
Magadha, one of the largest Indian kingdoms at that
time. Most representative of them were the free
thinkers referred to in Buddhist texts as the six non-
Buddhist teachers.

One of the six was the skeptic philosopher Sanjaya,
who held that, for the sake of personal liberation, it

was necessary to abandon ideas of another world or of cause and effect, since it is impossible to say whether such things do or do not exist. One of the foremost thinkers of the time, he had two hundred and fifty disciples.

But suddenly something totally unexpected happened. His two leading disciples, Sariputta and Moggallana, who were entrusted with supervising all the others, left their master, taking all the other followers with them, and went to another teacher.

That action was the result of the following course of events. Early one morning, while Sariputta was walking through the streets of Rajagaha, he came upon a mendicant monk who was begging for food. The monk held his alms bowl, walked quietly with downcast eyes, and deported himself with such propriety that Sariputta was strongly impressed.

He thought, "This monk must either have attained enlightenment himself or have taken as his teacher a perfectly enlightened person." Curious though he was, Sariputta suppressed his desire to speak to the monk and simply followed him.

When the monk had finished begging and had eaten his meal, Sariputta made a courteous bow and said, "Friend, your appearance is truly impressive. Who are you, and who is your teacher?"

The monk replied, "I have abandoned secular life to follow the great enlightened teacher who came from the land of the Shakyas. I am called Assaji."

Sariputta then asked, "What is the doctrine of this enlightened teacher of the Shakyas?"

"I cannot tell you in detail, since it has not been long since I became a monk and began serving him."

"The main points will be enough. What does your honored teacher proclaim?"

Assaji replied, "All things are produced by causation. The Buddha has explained the causes and the way to eliminate them. This is his teaching."

From that brief statement Sariputta, who was later to be known as foremost in wisdom among all Shakyamuni's followers, perceived the Way to supreme enlightenment and immortality. He realized clearly that this was the teaching he had long sought and that the teacher he had hoped for had at last appeared.

Born into a Brahman family in the village of Nalaka, not far from Rajagaha, Sariputta demonstrated exceptional intelligence from earliest childhood. He first studied with his father, who was widely versed in Brahmanic knowledge, and learned to recite the Vedas. At the age of eight he began formal study with a teacher, and by the time he was sixteen his fame had spread through the vicinity.

Not far from Nalaka was the village of Kolita, where Moggallana was born. He and Sariputta were to become the "two great jewels" of the Sangha. By coincidence they were born in neighboring villages and were friends from childhood.

Moggallana too was a boy of exceptional abilities. After he and Sariputta became close friends, they respected each other and sought the Way to enlightenment together. When the time came for them to leave the secular world for a life of religious pursuit, they also did so together.

One year, Sariputta and Moggallana joined the brilliantly arrayed crowd of people gathered to enjoy themselves and watch voluptuous dancing girls at Rajagaha's annual Mountaintop Festival. Gazing at the festivities, Sariputta was seized by an indescribable sense of futility and emptiness.

"Sooner or later," he said to his companion, "all these merrymakers must end their lives in this world. Not only the pleasure seekers but I too will meet the same fate. When death pursues, can it be right to squander time this way?" At that moment he determined to leave the secular world and devote himself to finding a way to liberation from a fate that makes death the end of everything. His friend Moggallana made the same decision.

Having gained their parents' permission, Sariputta and Moggallana abandoned secular life and visited the various teachers who expounded new doctrines in the city of Rajagaha. Sanjaya was the one they elected to follow.

Because of their outstanding abilities and learning, Sariputta and Moggallana were soon recognized as preeminent among his disciples. But even after mastering everything Sanjaya had to teach, they did not attain true enlightenment and continued to long for a teacher who could lead them to their goal. Probably it was their ardent wish for truth that created the opportunity for Sariputta to meet Assaji.

When Moggallana saw Sariputta trembling with emotion at having finally found the supreme teacher, he realized that Sariputta had discovered the way to true liberation. A long time earlier, the two men had agreed that should one discover the teaching that led to enlightenment, he would share it with the other. Honoring this promise, Sariputta immediately told Moggallana what he had heard. The two then resolved to put their faith in Shakyamuni. They told the rest of

Sanjaya's two hundred and fifty disciples of their decision, and all expressed the desire to follow Shakyamuni.

It is said that when Sariputta, Moggallana, and the others went to see Shakyamuni at the Bamboo Grove Monastery, outside Rajagaha, Shakyamuni said, "These two friends will become the two great jewels, the supreme among my disciples." This occurred the year after Shakyamuni's enlightenment, when Sariputta was twenty-seven or twenty-eight years of age.

Owing to his keen intelligence, after putting his faith in Shakyamuni, Sariputta is said to have mastered the teachings of causal origination, the Four Noble Truths, and the Eightfold Path and to have attained perfect enlightenment. In addition, he was able to expound the essence of Shakyamuni's teachings to others.

Once, while Sariputta was visiting Nalaka, a philosopher asked him to define nirvana.

Sariputta replied, "Friend, nirvana is the extinction of desire, anger, and ignorance."

The philosopher then asked how to attain nirvana.

Sariputta said, "Friend, the Eightfold Path set forth by our great teacher—right view, right thinking, right speech, right action, right livelihood, right endeavor, right mindfulness, and right meditation—is the way to attain nirvana."

Observing Sariputta teach the Dharma in this way, Shakyamuni said to his followers, "If you would leave the secular world and study the Way, you must be as Sariputta and Moggallana are. Take great pains to become close to them and entreat them to teach you."

Though Sariputta was recognized as one of the first of all the disciples and as a model of the self-disciplined monk, and though he was called on to teach the other monks in place of Shakyamuni himself, he never became self-important. On the contrary, after the others had gone out begging, he would go around their quarters putting everything in order. He is also said to have striven quietly to ensure that the Sangha did not invite criticism from other religious groups. Though a man of great intellect, he always showed compassionate consideration for others.

While begging in Rajagaha one day, he stopped at the gate of the home of a wealthy man. Just then the wealthy man's son came out and, seeing Sariputta, asked who he was and what teaching he followed.

Sariputta replied, "I am a disciple of Shakyamuni, the greatest teacher in the world."

The son asked again, "You have come with a mendicant's bowl. What do you seek?"

Sariputta replied, "I seek neither wealth, nor food, nor ornaments. I have come for your sake. You are fated to meet Shakyamuni. It is difficult to encounter a buddha who has come into the world to teach the Dharma. Come with me and pay reverence to him and hear his teachings." It is said that at Sariputta's urging this young man abandoned secular life to follow Shakyamuni.

No one in Savatthi, the capital of the kingdom of Kosala, had put faith in Shakyamuni's teachings until a wealthy merchant named Sudatta became a believer and donated a garden on the southern outskirts of the city to the Sangha. There Sariputta, entrusted with the important and difficult task of building a monastery in a land of other faiths, constructed the Jetavana Monastery to accommodate the Buddha and his followers when they visited the city.

After hearing Shakyamuni teach the Dharma at the new Jetavana Monastery, Sariputta happened upon a monk he had known before. The man asked Sariputta where he was coming from, and he replied, "I have just heard the teachings of Shakyamuni."

Smiling coldly, the monk retorted, "Are you still depending on teachers? I have long ago broken with them and am seeking the Way on my own."

Sariputta said, "A calf will abandon the frenzied mother cow after drinking only a little of her milk. Similarly, it is because your teacher has not attained correct enlightenment that you have left his side. Just as it is impossible to grow weary of the milk of a good, sound cow, so, because my great teacher has attained true enlightenment, his teachings are inexhaustible."

A model to all the other members of the Sangha, Sariputta put absolute faith in Shakyamuni and, according to tradition, entered the state of nirvana at his own request before his master did so. At the time of Sariputta's request to be permitted to enter nirvana, Shakyamuni was already eighty years of age and so gravely ill that he knew his own death and entrance into nirvana were near.

At first Shakyamuni made no answer; but after Sariputta had made the same request a second and then a third time, Shakyamuni said, "Why are you in such a hurry to enter nirvana?"

"You have already said that your own nirvana is near," answered Sariputta. "I cannot bear to see it. It is said that all the leading disciples of all the buddhas have entered nirvana before their masters. Please permit me to do as they have done." Shakyamuni nodded slightly.

Sariputta returned to his village, entered his family

home, and went to his room, where he said to the one follower he had brought with him, "I have been with all of you for more than forty years. If I have offended anyone, forgive me."

These were his last words. The scriptures say that toward evening that day he lay down on his bed and quietly entered nirvana.

MOGGALLANA
Foremost in Supernatural Powers

Moggallana, together with Sariputta, led Sanjaya's two hundred and fifty followers to become disciples of Shakyamuni. Moggallana and Sariputta were known as the pillars of the Sangha. Just as Sariputta was foremost in wisdom, so was Moggallana foremost in supernatural powers, manifestations of which are described in various scriptures. The best-known episode relating to his supernatural powers has to do with his mother's deliverance from hell.

Having acquired complete freedom in supernatural powers while studying and training under Shakyamuni at the Jetavana Monastery, Moggallana decided to use his powers to discover where his deceased mother had been reborn and to try to recompense her for her care in bringing him up. After many inquiries he finally learned that she was suffering in the hell of hungry demons. Upon learning this, Moggallana immediately used his supernatural powers to send her a bowl of food. She was overjoyed, but as soon as she tried to put the food into her mouth it burst into flames, causing her even greater pain than before.

Grieved by her plight, Moggallana asked Shakya-muni to save his mother. Shakyamuni replied, "Your power alone cannot atone for her sins. You must make offerings to all the monks and ask them to pray for her. Then their prayers will free your mother from the hell of hungry demons." Moggallana did as instructed, and the merit he obtained by making offerings to all the monks delivered his mother from hell.

In those days people who devoted their lives to religion undertook extremely strict training to attain a state of mental and spiritual unification and concentration. Having attained this state, a person became an *arahant* capable of doing wonderful things. For instance, *arahants* were endowed with highly sensitive faculties enabling them to see things ordinary people could not see, hear things they could not hear, read their minds, know their pasts, and act with perfect freedom. Though apparently miraculous, these powers were actually attained as a consequence of long training and discipline.

Sariputta was able to go directly to the heart of matters as a result of his great intellect. Moggallana, meanwhile, attained his extraordinary powers of perception through unrelenting will and vigorous effort. In comparison with Sariputta, a man of intellect, Moggallana was a man of practical action. The discipline to which he subjected himself after he and Sariputta became followers of Shakyamuni is said to have been astounding.

The village of Kolita, where Moggallana was born, was near Rajagaha and adjacent to the village of Nalaka, Sariputta's birthplace. As described in the story of Sariputta, Moggallana and Sariputta had been close friends since childhood and respected each other deeply. Moggallana's family, for generations Brahman instructors to kings, lived in a mansion that is said to have been comparable in size to the royal palace in Rajagaha. After discussions with Sariputta, Moggallana decided to abandon secular life for the life of religion. At first his distinguished family objected fiercely, since the outstanding abilities that even in early childhood had won Moggallana renown in neighboring villages had given his family great hopes for him. Nonetheless, his parents knew their son well and were aware of his unusual strength of will and depth of thought; they realized that he must have given the matter profound consideration and that his decision was firm.

After finally persuading his parents, Moggallana, together with Sariputta, became a follower of Sanjaya the skeptic. Later the two men chose Shakyamuni as their teacher and joined the Sangha. Moggallana left the Bamboo Grove Monastery outside Rajagaha, where Shakyamuni was staying at the time, and went to nearby Vulture Peak, where he sat in a cave and submitted himself to the strictest discipline in order to attain the state of concentration in which neither perception nor thought occurs.

During this course of training Moggallana refused to allow himself to sleep or even to rest. When he became discouraged, Shakyamuni, who was actually at the Bamboo Grove Monastery, would appear before him to encourage him to persevere. On one occasion Moggallana went to a certain village to meditate but was so weary that he soon fell asleep. Shakyamuni appeared before him and said, "Moggallana, do not covet sleep. Recite the Dharma. Transmit the Dharma to other people. He who would expound the Dharma must abandon, eliminate, and destroy his own strength." No doubt Moggallana's great desire for enlightenment conveyed itself to Shakyamuni, who was some distance away, and caused him to appear before his disciple. When Moggallana's discipline finally brought him enlightenment, he is reported to have said, "I have been enlightened because of my master's teachings and encouragement. I have, therefore, been born of my master."

Because of his devotion to Shakyamuni, Moggallana must have been able to see his gentle face and hear his voice all the time he was meditating to attain spiritual unification. Even after that training for enlightenment had ended, he was still able to make contact with Shakyamuni no matter what distance separated them. Shakyamuni once went to the Jetavana Monastery, leaving Moggallana and Sariputta behind at the Bamboo Grove Monastery. One day while Shakyamuni was away Moggallana turned to Sariputta and said he had just spoken with Shakyamuni. In amazement Sariputta said, "How could you have spoken with him when he is far away, beyond rivers and mountains, at the Jetavana Monastery?" Moggallana replied, "It is not that I have used my supernatural powers to go to his side or that he has used his to come to me. But with my supernatural powers of sight and hearing, I spoke to him and he replied, expounding diligence to me."

Hearing this, Sariputta said in praise, "My friend, all of us who seek the Way must respect you, be close to you, and make all efforts to become like you, as the small stone nearby resembles the great mountains of the Himalayas."

Moggallana was equally generous in praising his friend Sariputta. On one occasion, having heard

Sariputta eloquently expound the four ways to liberation, Moggallana exclaimed in admiration, "Friend, your teachings are like food to the hungry and water to the thirsty."

These two men, born in neighboring villages, followed the same teacher and, each regarding the other as a mirror of himself, strove to perfect their own innate characteristics. Realizing their effort, Shakyamuni praised them to the other monks: "Sariputta is like the mother who gives birth in that he awakens in the mind the desire to seek the Way. Moggallana is like the mother who rears the child in that he cultivates the mind to go on seeking the Way. All monks who discipline themselves should take these two men as examples and strive to emulate them in perfecting themselves." The other monks loved Sariputta for his compassionate concern for them and revered Moggallana for protecting them from the criticisms of other religious groups and for keeping a watchful eye on Shakyamuni's lay disciples.

As the years passed, the number of people professing faith in Shakyamuni's teachings increased. They included wealthy people in many lands and even Pasenadi, king of Kosala, and Bimbisara, king of Magadha. But the increasing prosperity of the Sangha also drew envy and ill will from followers of other religions. Moggallana, who had always openly expounded the teachings of Shakyamuni and opposed other beliefs, was often the object of persecution. On one occasion members of a rival religious group plotted to disgrace Moggallana by having a prostitute named Uppalavanna seduce him. Uppalavanna had been through two unhappy marriages through no fault of her own. With his supernatural powers Moggallana perceived her desperation and led her to faith in the Buddha's teachings.

In the end, though, Moggallana was killed by his persecutors. Religious rivals hired ruffians to attack him as he meditated in the mountains. According to the scriptures, though stoned until his bones were broken, he nonetheless managed to return to the Bamboo Grove Monastery, where he declared, "I can no longer tolerate this pain and will now enter nirvana." With these words he died.

Shakyamuni, who had already announced the imminence of his own entrance into nirvana, must have grieved greatly at the death of Moggallana. Just as great, if not greater, must have been the grief of Sariputta at the loss of the irreplaceable friend with whom he had sought the Way and with whom he had vowed to serve Shakyamuni. For him Moggallana's death must have been like his own. And indeed it was not long afterward that Sariputta, having obtained the permission of his master Shakyamuni, entered nirvana himself.

MAHA-KASSAPA
Foremost in Ascetic Practices

Maha-Kassapa is said to have become a disciple of Shakyamuni shortly after Sariputta and Moggallana. He is called Maha-Kassapa, or Great Kassapa, to distinguish him from other disciples named Kassapa.

The story of how Maha-Kassapa gave up secular life to seek religious truth resembles the course of events that inspired Shakyamuni himself to leave his father's palace in Kapilavatthu and devote himself to religion. Maha-Kassapa was born in a village near Rajagaha into a Brahman family so wealthy that it had twenty-five storehouses filled with gold, silver, and other valuables and cultivated more land than the king himself. He was reared in the innermost part of the family mansion, with four nurses to tend to his every need.

Extremely talented from early youth, by the age of eight he had mastered the rules of Brahman religious practice and was diligently applying himself to such pursuits as painting, dance, and mathematics. Gradually, however, he became so alienated from his life of luxury and from people driven solely by the desire for wealth and glory that he resolved to abandon it all someday for a life of religious pursuit.

Observing how little pleasure he took in anything, his parents began to worry. Fearing that he would leave home to devote himself to religion, they decided he should marry and settle down. Maha-Kassapa shrank from their almost daily urgings to wed, but they continued to plead with him to do as they wished and fulfill his duties as heir. At his wits' end, Maha-Kassapa finally had a sculptor mold a supremely noble and beautiful female figure in pure gold. Showing it to his parents, he said, "If you can find a woman as lovely as this, I promise to make her my wife." Though they feared that they would never find a woman as lovely as the statue, his parents searched the land and finally found a woman identical in every feature to the gold sculpture. Maha-Kassapa had no choice but to keep his promise.

The wedding safely concluded, his relieved parents happily awaited the birth of a grandchild. But no child was born. Nor is this surprising, since the young couple never so much as touched each other, for the woman Maha-Kassapa had married was completely free of ordinary human desires. Finally Maha-Kassapa's parents died without a grandchild. Because the family's immense wealth could not merely be abandoned, Maha-Kassapa was compelled to become head of the household. But before long something happened that showed him that people cannot escape repeated sin until they abandon the world.

One day, observing workers in his family's fields, he saw how the spade turned up earth teeming with white insects, which were crushed to death in the next instant by blows of the hoe. He saw how the farmers whipped groaning oxen that were forced to pull heavy loads. Through these images Maha-Kassapa came to understand the transience of life and the great suffering required to support his life of luxury. The same day, Maha-Kassapa's wife saw with horror how countless tiny insects were killed in the process of pressing sesame oil.

That evening, Maha-Kassapa said to his wife, "As long as my mother and father were alive, I suppressed my longing to leave secular life because I could not bear to make them unhappy. But now this way of life has become like a prison to me, and I wish to devote myself exclusively to religion." His wife made no objection, since she shared his feelings.

The scriptures say that Maha-Kassapa made the following comment at the time of his decision: "A layman's way of life is filled with obstructions and rubbish. A monk's life, in contrast, is as open and pleasant as the sky itself. It is difficult while living in a house to perform purifying deeds that gleam like pearls. I will therefore leave my house, shave my head, don a monk's robe, and devote myself to the search for truth." With that, Maha-Kassapa gave up his wealth to search for a teacher and eternal happiness.

One day Shakyamuni was resting in the shade of a tree beside a road in the village of Nalanda, not far from Rajagaha. Maha-Kassapa, who was passing by, stopped to look at this man, whom he did not remember having seen before but whose face was filled with compassion, purity, and nobility. Making up his mind at once that this was the person he wanted as his teacher and master, he fell at Shakyamuni's feet and asked if he might become one of his disciples.

Shakyamuni replied, "The head of a man revered

as a teacher who claims to know what he does not know and to have seen what he has not seen will split into seven parts like a fig. But put your mind at rest: I am not such a person." Then, as his first teaching to Maha-Kassapa, he said, "You must think correctly all the time and thoroughly grasp the nature of all things in the world as they inevitably come into and go out of existence."

As soon as Maha-Kassapa had been accepted as a disciple, he folded his own garment, made a cushion of it, and invited the Buddha to sit on it. When he did so, the Buddha commented on the pleasant softness of the cloth. Noticing that the Buddha wore a shabby robe of stitched-together rags, Maha-Kassapa begged him to accept his own robe. The Buddha did so and offered his own ragged garment in return to Maha-Kassapa, who was overcome with gratitude.

From that time on, Maha-Kassapa devoted himself to the life of an ascetic. He said, "The ascetic lives in the forest. Since he knows that accepting offerings from good houses pollutes him, he eats only what he obtains by begging and wears only rags, but must consider this way of life pleasant."

For a man who had formerly lived in comfort, waited on by servants, it must have been unimaginably difficult to beg from door to door. Yet Maha-Kassapa never flinched from it, as the following passage from the *Theragatha* reveals: "Once, leaving my lodging, I entered a city to beg. I approached and respectfully stood by a leper who was eating. With his rotting hand, the man offered me some rice. As he was placing it into my bowl, one of his fingers dropped off and fell into the bowl. But I ate that rice and neither then nor thereafter felt any disgust."

As the number of lay believers wanting to hear the Buddha's teachings increased, more and more offerings were made to the Sangha, and the monks were able to wear finer garments. Never deviating from his ascetic path, however, Maha-Kassapa continued to wear only robes made of rags. Other members of the Sangha began to whisper behind his back and to criticize him for his unsightly appearance when better clothing was available. No doubt to rebuke these monks, one day Shakyamuni prepared a place beside his own and invited Maha-Kassapa to sit there. Then he said to everyone, "Maha-Kassapa's ascetic practices in no way differ from my own self-discipline."

Even in old age, Maha-Kassapa continued to increase the rigor of his asceticism, so much so that Shakyamuni began to worry about his health and one day said to him, "Maha-Kassapa, you are no longer young. Walking about in those ragged garments must be difficult for you. Why not change them for the soft, light garments rich people donate? And instead of begging, accept donations from the wealthy. Don't sleep at night under trees anymore. From now on, stay by my side."

Tears rising in his eyes at the thought of the Buddha's concern for his welfare, Maha-Kassapa said, "Master, I still have the ragged garment you gave me when I first became a monk. I have never worn anything softer than the master's robe. My daily food has always been what I obtained by begging. I have sought the Way thus to avoid losing the spiritual attitude I had when I began this kind of life. But I have regarded the ascetic way of life not as suffering but as happiness, because it brings the unsurpassed joy of wanting little and knowing sufficiency."

The Buddha responded, "Maha-Kassapa, you have spoken well and will be a light to people who come after you. Through the model of your unflagging discipline, many will find happiness." And until his death, Maha-Kassapa continued to require no more than was actually necessary to sustain life.

After the Buddha's death, Maha-Kassapa presided over the First Council, at which Shakyamuni's teachings were compiled. He continued to expound these teachings until his death, serving as a model for those devoting themselves to ascetic practices.

UPALI
Foremost in Keeping the Precepts

Six young nobles of the Shakya tribe—Ananda, Anuruddha, Bhaddiya, Bhagu, Devadatta, and Kimbila—resolved together to become Shakyamuni's disciples. When they left the kingdom's capital, Kapilavatthu, it was with such a great train of carts, horses, elephants, and retainers that everyone thought they were embarking on an excursion. At the boundary between the land of the Shakyas and the kingdom of Magadha, however, they sent their entire train back to the capital, keeping with them only Upali, a barber.

In a grove on the border, they ordered Upali to shave their heads. Next they removed their rich clothes and jeweled ornaments and put on the coarse garments they had prepared. They then said to the barber, "Upali, you have served us long and well. We have made up our minds to go to Anupiya, in the kingdom of Malla, where Shakyamuni is staying, and ask him to include us among his disciples. Since we are going to renounce the secular world, these clothes and ornaments are no longer of any use to us. Take them all and return quickly with them to Kapilavatthu."

Upali stared after the young nobles as they vanished

into the forest. Then, coming to himself, he was overwhelmed by the heap of costly things lying at his feet.
Trembling, he picked them up and hastily concealed
himself in the woods, where he puzzled over the meaning of what had just happened. He thought, "There
can be no doubt that I have been given great wealth,
enough to feed me for the rest of my life." But he at
once saw that if he took the riches home, people would
suspect him of having stolen them. To a man like
Upali, who had always been honest, being the object
of such suspicions would have been intolerable. Even
if he reported what had happened, he would probably
be punished for having aided the young nobles in abandoning secular life for the life of religion. Upali was at
his wits' end.

Then he began wondering why the six young men
had given up their lives of wealth and comfort to
devote themselves to religion. He suddenly recalled
words he had heard a few days earlier at the Nigrodha
Monastery, outside Kapilavatthu: "All the suffering of
the world is born of greed. Unless greed is abandoned,
true peace of mind is impossible to attain." The
speaker had been Shakyamuni, who had once been the
Shakya crown prince but had left home to search for
the Way to perfect enlightenment.

Upali immediately saw that the cause of his confusion and fear was the desire that had awakened in him
as soon as he had received the nobles' belongings.
"Now I understand," he exclaimed to himself.
"Those young men left the secular world in the hope
of finding peace of mind." He realized that Shakyamuni was a great person, able to see the innermost
recesses of the human heart. Upali resolved to ask
the young men to take him with them to Shakya-

muni. No longer interested in the garments and jewels, he hung them on trees, one to a branch. Praying that some pure-hearted traveler would find and be made happy by the riches, he hastened after the nobles.

That decision required great determination. The barber Upali, who was later to be revered as preeminent in keeping the precepts, had been born into the lowest of the four major castes, which were rigidly fixed in the time of Shakyamuni. People born into one of these castes—the Brahmans at the top, followed by the Kshatriyas, Vaishyas, and Sudras—remained in it for life. Those in the lowest caste had no hope of improving their status, regardless of ability. Members of the Sudra caste, like Upali, were not permitted to eat with, much less fraternize with or marry, members of the caste to which the nobles belonged.

Thinking Upali had returned to Kapilavatthu, the young men were surprised to see him in pursuit and asked him what was the matter. What had happened to the clothes and jewelry they had given him? Had he been set upon by robbers? Panting, Upali replied, "No. Please listen to what I have to say. Riches of that kind are not suitable for a poor man like me. First of all, they would disturb my peace of mind. Be good enough to take me with you to Shakyamuni." They did as he asked, and thus the six young nobles and Upali the barber made obeisance together at the feet of the Buddha.

The Buddha asked the six young nobles who the man behind them was and was told that he was Upali the barber, who though of low birth had served the Shakyas well. Stiff with fear, Upali advanced timidly. Shakyamuni gently asked if he was seeking the Way.

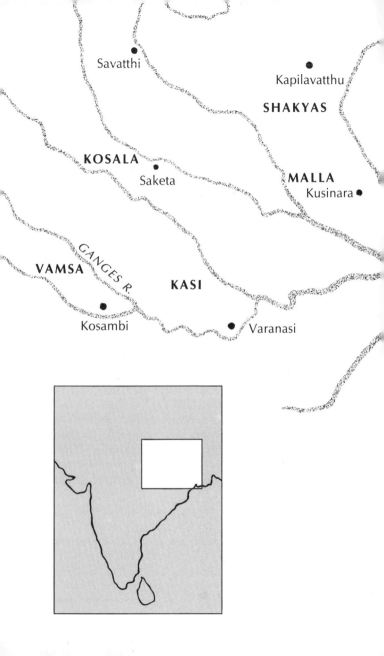

The India of the Buddha

VAJJI CONFEDERATION

• Vesali

Pataliputta (Patna)
●

GANGES R.

● Rajagaha (Rajgir)

Champa ●

● Gaya

ANGA

MAGADHA

MAGADHA	Ancient states
Rajagaha	Ancient place names
(Rajgir)	Modern place names

(Calcutta) ●

Upali replied, "Yes, if a person of mean birth like me can be permitted to become a monk."

With a deep nod, Shakyamuni said, "Upali, people are not valuable because of birth. Put your mind at rest. Our Sangha makes no distinction on the basis of occupation or social class. The only rank that exists is seniority in the Sangha itself. Receive your ordination now."

The six young nobles were astounded that Upali should be ordained ahead of them, since this would mean they would be in a lower position than he and would have to pay reverence to him. One of them voiced their general discontent: "But Upali was our servant. . . ."

Shakyamuni replied crisply, "Why should people who have left secular life to be free of the desires of the world persist in clinging to discrimination by social class? That is not how you should seek the Way."

Having been a prince himself, Shakyamuni no doubt saw the conceit of these young men, who formerly had commanded the services of hordes of underlings. It was to awaken them to their own pride that he ordained Upali ahead of them. It is said that the young men recognized the meaning of the Buddha's act and paid sincere reverence to Upali after he was ordained, taking places inferior to his.

One scripture offers the following account of why Upali was able to overcome his lowly birth to become one of the Buddha's disciples. When Shakyamuni was a hermit in an earlier existence, he once asked the palace barber to shave his head, but the barber refused contemptuously because of the hermit's wretched appearance. The barber's nephew, who was an inexperienced novice, condemned his uncle's unkindness and did his best to shave the hermit. The young man revered the hermit thereafter and prayed to be reborn as a barber serving him in a future life, in which he would continue to seek the Way. This man was Upali in an earlier existence.

Neither proud nor servile, always accepting frankly what people said and doing all things sincerely, Upali learned and kept all the precepts so well that he surpassed all other members of the Sangha in this endeavor.

Upali once asked for permission to retire to the seclusion of the forests to train himself in meditative concentration, but Shakyamuni replied, "Each person has his own abilities. You are not made for the solitude of the forests. Let us imagine a huge elephant bathing happily in a lake. What would happen if a rabbit or a cat, observing the elephant's enjoyment, tried to emulate it by jumping into the water?" Upali then realized that he should remain in the Sangha, devoting himself to discipline and training, keeping the precepts, and serving as a guide to the other monks. Whenever he entertained the least doubt on some point, he immediately referred the question to the Buddha. He kept all the precepts—beginning of course with the five basic ones of not taking life, stealing, indulging in sexual misconduct, lying, or drinking intoxicants—so well that other people began coming to him for advice on them.

It must not be thought, however, that Upali followed the precepts dogmatically. He knew how to make exceptions. Once he met a sick old monk who was returning from a journey. Hearing that the old man's illness could be cured by drinking wine, Upali went to his master and asked what he should do. The Buddha said that sick people were exempt from the precept forbidding the drinking of intoxicants. Upali immediately gave wine to the old man, who recovered.

Upali observed the precepts for the sake of all the monks and for the improvement of the Sangha. He was revered for the way in which he resolved the disputes that frequently disturbed the Sangha, and after the Buddha's death he contributed greatly to the successful transmission of the Buddha's teachings to later generations by authenticating the precepts at the First Council, which met to compile the Buddha's teachings.

ANANDA
Foremost in Hearing Many Teachings

Ananda, whose name appears in many scriptures, served Shakyamuni for years as a personal attendant, seldom leaving his side. Because he had so many opportunities to hear the Buddha speak and because he understood and recalled perfectly what he heard, he was known as foremost in hearing many teachings.

Ananda and his older brother, Devadatta, who would become infamous for his attempts to disrupt the Sangha and for his many assaults on the Buddha, were among the group of six young Shakya nobles who, with the barber Upali, together requested permission to join the Sangha. Although Upali and the others received their ordinations immediately, Ananda and Devadatta were not permitted to do so.

At the time, many young Shakya aristocrats from the city of Kapilavatthu were abandoning secular life for the life of religion. Ananda had requested his parents' permission to do the same, but owing to his mother's intense love for him and her dread of losing him, permission had been denied. One night, gathering his valuables together, Ananda left home to study with a hermit in Videha. Hearing that Ananda had left home and taken a vow of silence, his mother realized that she was powerless to stop him and finally gave him permission to follow the religious life.

Upon learning this, Ananda immediately went to Devadatta, who had asked Ananda to take him along when he went to join the Sangha. Devadatta had already asked to be allowed to join once but had been refused. Shakyamuni had told him he was unsuited to a life of religious discipline and should remain at home, accumulate wealth, and acquire merit through charitable works. Nonetheless, Devadatta decided that if Ananda was going, he too would try again.

Together with four other Shakya nobles, Ananda and Devadatta went to the place where Shakyamuni was staying. But Ananda and Devadatta were discouraged when their request to enter the Sangha was rejected. They then became disciples of an ascetic under whom they trained in a forest near the Bamboo Grove Monastery, but they could not rid their minds of the noble image of the Buddha. After a while Ananda and Devadatta approached Shakyamuni again, made obeisance to him by touching their foreheads to his feet, and repeated their request: "Please admit us into the Sangha. We will follow any discipline imposed on us and will never depart from your teachings." No doubt taking pity on them because of the desperate expression on Ananda's face and lending an ear to other members of the Sangha who urged their acceptance, the Buddha assented and the two were ordained.

From that day forward, Ananda devoted himself to training and discipline. But by nature a gentle, sympathetic person, he found breaking with the delusions of the world very difficult. It was probably because

Shakyamuni had perceived that Ananda was innately ill suited to a life of severe religious discipline and had wished to make Ananda realize this for himself that he had at first refused to grant Ananda's request to enter the Sangha. But Ananda made great efforts to overcome his weaknesses.

After some time had passed, Shakyamuni spoke one day to a gathering of disciples including Sariputta, Moggallana, Maha-Kassapa, and other senior monks at the Bamboo Grove Monastery. He said, "I am now in my mid-fifties and am weak and unable to do everything for myself. I need an attendant. Would you choose one for me?"

The senior monks were deeply moved to see how weary Shakyamuni had grown from severe discipline and strenuous teaching. One of them, named Kondanna, stepped forward and expressed willingness to assume the responsibility. With deep compassion, Shakyamuni looked into his upturned, expectant face and said, "Kondanna, I am pleased by your offer, but you are as old as I and need an attendant yourself."

One by one Sariputta, Moggallana, Maha-Kassapa, Kacchayana, and the other senior monks offered to serve as attendant, but Shakyamuni declined all their offers. Then Moggallana, foremost in supernatural powers, suddenly realized that Shakyamuni had already selected the person he wanted to serve him. Immediately entering a state of profound meditative concentration, he saw what was in the Buddha's mind: the figure of the young monk Ananda. Emerging from his state of meditation, he went at once to the grove where the young man was meditating and told him that he should serve as Shakyamuni's attendant.

Ananda replied that it was unthinkable that a person

with so few qualifications should perform such a service for the Buddha, the supreme teacher. Moggallana replied, "Ananda, listen well. Shakyamuni wants you to serve him. Even knowing that, do you refuse?"

A great joy welled up in Ananda's heart at the news that Shakyamuni, who had found the Way, knew the true nature of all things, and was endowed with all wisdom and virtue, should have chosen him, immature as he was, to be his attendant. In the next instant, however, he reproved himself for his elation and told himself that he could not carry out the great task facing him unless he was sober in his thinking. He saw that he would have to be pure in mind and restrained in body.

Accompanied by Moggallana, Ananda approached Shakyamuni and requested that the Buddha hear the three vows he had made. Shakyamuni assented, and Ananda said, "First, I vow never to accept any garments from the master. Second, I will never sit in any place prepared in homage to the master. Third, I vow never to enter the master's presence except at appointed times. Please hear these three vows that I have made in my heart."

Ananda had realized that the other members of the Sangha and lay believers might accord him special deference because he would be by the Buddha's side. Aware of his own immaturity in training and discipline, he had resolved to be discreet, avoid pride, and never stray from the true path. The Buddha nodded upon hearing the vows that resulted from this determination. From that day until the Buddha's death, twenty-five years later, Ananda served his master faithfully and was always with him. It is said that he was chosen for this task at the age of twenty-five, five years after he had become a member of the Sangha.

Rather than merely follow Shakyamuni's instructions, Ananda heard many teachings, understood and remembered them all, and sometimes requested guidance from the Buddha on his own initiative. Once, in the village of Sakkhara in the kingdom of the Shakyas, he asked the Buddha whether association with good friends was of value in pursuing the Way. Shakyamuni replied, "Ananda, association with good friends is the whole Way." Suddenly Ananda realized that the Buddha, having liberated himself from all desires and attained perfect enlightenment, was pursuing the Way in the company of his friends, including Ananda himself and the other members of the Sangha.

Shakyamuni—then known as Siddhattha—had been reared by his aunt Mahapajapati after the early death of his mother, Maya. When his father, King Suddhodana, died, she requested permission to join the Sangha. At first Shakyamuni refused because she was a woman. It is said that Ananda pleaded with the Buddha to allow women to become members of the Sangha. A central figure in the founding of the women's Sangha, Ananda earned the respect of the many women who became nuns. In fact, Ananda's compassionate nature and engaging personality attracted everyone. And because of his gentle and beautiful face, women often became infatuated with him. Once he even had to be saved from the danger of seduction by Shakyamuni's supernatural powers.

Ananda suffered greatly when Shakyamuni, eighty years old and ill, approached the hour of his death. In accordance with custom, at the start of the rainy season Shakyamuni and Ananda had stopped traveling and taken up residence on the outskirts of Vesali, the capital of the Vajji confederation. As Ananda looked after Shakyamuni's needs, he began to fear that his master would die soon. But Ananda believed that Shakyamuni would not leave the Sangha without final instructions. Diligently fulfilling his duties, Ananda watched Shakyamuni slowly recover. When Ananda asked Shakyamuni about the possibility of his dying without saying something in farewell to the monks and nuns, Shakyamuni told him, "I have already revealed all the teachings; nothing remains for me to explain. Ananda, do not grieve for me after my death. When I have departed, rely on yourself, rely on the Dharma, and be diligent in following the Way."

Resuming his travels after the rainy season, Shakyamuni came to the village of Pava, in the kingdom of Malla. After eating a meal offered him by a local blacksmith named Chunda, he fell seriously ill again. Nevertheless, he continued his journey; but by the time he reached Kusinara his reserves of strength were exhausted. He quietly instructed Ananda to spread his bedding and lay down with his head to the north. Realizing that Shakyamuni's death was near, Ananda wept bitterly, but Shakyamuni said to him, "Ananda, you have served me well. Do not grieve. Though I disappear from this world, I live forever. Follow my instructions, keep the teachings and the precepts diligently, and find perfect enlightenment as soon as possible."

Ananda took this counsel to heart and, as a result of his diligence, finally attained enlightenment after the Buddha's death. At the time of the First Council he performed a key service in the compilation of the scriptures by reciting all the teachings he had heard from Shakyamuni.

ANURUDDHA
Foremost in Divine Insight

After attaining enlightenment under the *bodhi* tree at Gaya, in the kingdom of Magadha, Shakyamuni traveled through much of northeastern India teaching, and visited his home city of Kapilavatthu several times. The fame of the Buddha and his teaching of a way to eliminate suffering grew rapidly, and many young men of the Shakya tribe abandoned secular life to join the Sangha.

Anuruddha, Shakyamuni's cousin, who was later to be praised as foremost in divine insight, was a son of the Shakya royal house. One day, when everyone in Kapilavatthu was eagerly awaiting the arrival of the man whose teachings had won over so many young men in the capital, Anuruddha was visited by his older brother, Mahanama, who proposed that one of them give up secular life in the hope of gaining religious merit and that the other accept the responsibilities of heir to the family. Mahanama made this proposal because he was concerned that if both were to give up secular life no one would remain to carry on the family line. Anuruddha had no objection to his brother's proposal but was uncertain whether he, accustomed as he was to luxury and the freedom to do as he liked, could withstand the rigorous discipline of the religious life. If he took over the family responsibilities, on the other hand, he would spend the rest of his life coping with the constant demands of farming and of conducting Brahman religious ceremonies. He was torn between the two courses.

Anuruddha was aristocratic in appearance, with straight brows and a finely shaped nose, and was also skilled in martial arts and sports. His parents doted on him and gave him a house for each of the seasons—one for summer, one for winter, and one for the rainy season—just as Shakyamuni's parents had done for him when he was still Prince Siddhattha. In the inner apartments of these buildings Anuruddha had been carefully reared, attended by many serving women.

In spite of the comfort and luxury of his life, however, Anuruddha was dissatisfied. His life began to seem empty, and he was overcome by a profound sadness. During one of Shakyamuni's visits to Kapila-vatthu, Anuruddha caught a glimpse of this man who was pure and free of all the troubles of the world. That glimpse caused him to choose the life of religious pursuit.

He thought, "Shakyamuni felt more deeply than anyone the emptiness and futility of life in this world and sought liberation from suffering, a state of absolute tranquillity. He will be able to teach me how to find what I seek."

His mind made up, Anuruddha obtained permission from his older brother to join the Sangha and then went to his mother for her permission. She loved him deeply and refused at first; finally, however, seeing that he was resolute, she compromised and agreed to consent if Anuruddha's cousin Bhaddiya would also devote himself to the pursuit of religious truth. She felt safe in making that concession, since Bhaddiya had become king of the Shakyas after the death of King Suddhodana, Shakyamuni's father. It was unlikely that a man in such a position would discard his responsibilities and become a monk.

Anuruddha then went to Bhaddiya and requested his company in leaving the secular world to follow Shakyamuni. Torn between his state duties and his desire to become a monk, Bhaddiya first said he would accompany Anuruddha if he agreed to wait seven years. Anuruddha refused. The length of time was shortened to six years, then five, four, and so on to one year. Finally Bhaddiya promised to become a monk if Anuruddha waited a mere seven days.

Having persuaded Bhaddiya, Anuruddha went on to win over four more young nobles—Ananda, Bhagu, Devadatta, and Kimbila—and all of them, with the barber Upali, went to Shakyamuni and joined the Sangha.

Before becoming a monk, Anuruddha had worn beautiful clothes, slept on the softest bedding, and lived in comfort surrounded by servants. Now he found that wearing ragged robes, begging for food, sleeping outside, and other aspects of his new life of severe discipline were very difficult. But with stubborn perseverance, he finally became accustomed to the life of a monk, only to be assaulted by the fatigue brought on by such strict training.

One day, when he and many other disciples had gathered at the Jetavana Monastery to hear Shakyamuni teach, Anuruddha was overcome by drowsiness and fell asleep. He awoke with a start when he heard Shakyamuni call his name. Shakyamuni said, "It must be a pure and wise person who can take joy in hearing the Dharma and sleep peacefully, with no mental disturbance."

Those words, no doubt intended as a mild reproof, pierced the heart of the exhausted disciple. When the sermon ended, Anuruddha approached Shakyamuni, who said to him, "Why did you give up a regal life for the life of religious discipline? To escape the irksome duties of the crown? From fear of robbers?"

Overcome by shame, Anuruddha replied, "No, revered teacher. I did so to pursue the Way that transcends the suffering of birth, aging, illness, death, and all the other sorrows of the world."

"And do you think dozing will help you fulfill your wish?" asked Shakyamuni. Anuruddha realized that the indolent habits of court life still lingered deep in his mind and body, ready to rise to the surface at the least mental laxness.

Anuruddha said, "Revered teacher, I have been guilty of misconduct. Please forgive me. Never again will I sleep in front of you, not even if my eyes should melt and my body break out in sores." There was a look of extraordinary resolution on Anuruddha's face as he made this vow.

After making his vow of sleeplessness, Anuruddha began a fierce battle with his body's need for sleep. He is said to have gone for nights on end without closing his eyes. A long period of this severe discipline enabled him to attain the enlightenment of an *arahant,* but the strain caused his sight to fail. Shakyamuni instructed Anuruddha to consult a physician, who pronounced that he could be cured by sleep.

Shakyamuni, hearing this, called Anuruddha to his side and said, "By carrying out your vow, you have rid yourself of all delusions. Why not sleep peacefully now? As the body requires food for nourishment, so the eyes require sleep."

Deeply moved though he was by this demonstration of affection and compassion, Anuruddha replied, "Revered teacher, by making a vow of sleeplessness I have conquered suffering. How can I discard that vow now?"

Anuruddha knew how difficult it is for people to change their personalities and habits. An instant's inattention had allowed lethargy and pride to take over and had made him doze in the presence of the Buddha. He never forgot that incident or ceased to reproach himself for it. It was his burning desire for self-improvement and religious insight, not stubborn insistence on fulfilling his vow, that made him keep his vow of sleeplessness, even if it meant going blind. Indeed, Anuruddha finally did go blind. But as he lost physical sight he gained spiritual vision into the true nature of all things and came to be respected as foremost in divine insight.

On one occasion when a large number of disciples had gathered at the Jetavana Monastery to hear Shakyamuni teach, Anuruddha suddenly became aware of the ragged condition of his robe and wanted to mend it; but being blind, he could not thread the needle. He turned to the other monks nearby and said, "Would some monk who wishes to acquire merit and attain enlightenment thread this needle for me?"

A person approached and asked to be allowed to do the task, but Anuruddha recognized the voice of

Shakyamuni and said in surprise, "Revered teacher, I could not allow you to do it. I was thinking of a person who wanted to acquire merit and seek happiness."

To this Shakyamuni said, "No one in this world seeks happiness more than I."

"I do not like to appear to talk back to you, but you are a buddha. What Dharma can you seek beyond what you have already attained?" asked Anuruddha.

Shakyamuni answered, "Anuruddha, I too am continually seeking the Dharma. There is no end to seeking the Dharma, even for a buddha." Then he threaded the needle for Anuruddha, whose blind eyes filled with the radiant image of the Buddha.

RAHULA
Foremost in Quietly Doing Good

Rahula, Shakyamuni's only child, was born while his father was still Prince Siddhattha of the Shakyas. Siddhattha was nineteen when, at the instigation of his father, King Suddhodana, he married Yasodhara. Early in life Siddhattha became aware of the suffering inherent in birth into this world and spent more and more of his time wrapped in the contemplation of liberation from suffering. His desire to seek an end to suffering grew ever stronger. King Suddhodana had arranged the marriage with Yasodhara in the hope of preventing his heir from abandoning the secular world for a life of religious pursuit. No doubt the king was overjoyed to hear that after ten years of marriage Yasodhara had given birth to a son. He imagined that this would change Siddhattha's mind about leaving home. Upon hearing of the event, however, Siddhattha cried out, "A hindrance [*rahula*] has been born; bonds of affection have been created!" This is said to be why he named his son Rahula.

At that time India was torn by violent battles among great kingdoms. The strong constantly threatened the weak, and some people rejected the validity of morality. They claimed that there was no evil in taking life, stealing, or causing others suffering, since no retribution for deeds done in this world waited in the world to come. Many eagerly accepted this doctrine. Prince Siddhattha witnessed this world firsthand and foresaw clearly the downfall of his society. He resolved to find a way to lead people from unhappiness as quickly as possible.

The birth of a son must have been a tremendous cause of concern to the prince. Seven days after Rahula came into the world, Siddhattha broke the bonds of affection tying him to the infant and silently left the palace for a life of religious pursuit. To Yasodhara, who had lost her husband, and to Suddhodana, who had lost his son, Rahula must truly have been a child of sorrow. But this may have made them treat him all the more tenderly. Surrounded with affection, Rahula grew rapidly.

After Prince Siddhattha left home to pursue a life of religion, not a day passed that Yasodhara did not worry about the harsh suffering that her husband must be enduring. He had been accustomed to the softest cushions and many attendants. Now he slept in open fields and submitted himself to all kinds of ascetic hardships. Finally word reached her one day that Siddhattha had attained enlightenment and become a buddha. Soon afterward she learned that he was returning to visit Kapilavatthu, the capital.

He arrived in the company of a large number of disciples. They stayed in a forest outside the city, but paid a visit to King Suddhodana at the palace. During this visit Yasodhara pointed out the Buddha to Rahula and said, "That noble person is your father." Rahula advanced and looked up at his father, who returned his gaze but departed without saying a word.

Yasodhara hurried to her son and urged him to ask his father's blessing. Rahula did as he was told. Shakyamuni, turning back to look at his son, nodded and instructed the boy to follow as he continued walking. The boy did so in silence. When they reached the forest, Shakyamuni ordered Sariputta to shave Rahula's head, exchange his clothes for those of a monk, and make him a novice in the Sangha. Rahula is said to have been nine at the time.

Perhaps Shakyamuni foresaw the imminent fall of the Shakya tribe to one of the larger Indian kingdoms of the day. He must have realized how profoundly Yasodhara would suffer when her only son was taken away to lead a life of religious pursuit. No doubt he found it wrenching to tear his own child away from the comfort and wealth of life in the palace and compel him to wear the coarse robe of a monk and become a mendicant. Nonetheless, he was determined to give his son the precious legacy of enlightenment—eternal life and peace—attained only through strict religious discipline. Rahula's task was to follow the Way to its completion; and as a consequence of his actions, his mother too would eventually be brought to enlightenment.

As a member of the Sangha, Rahula underwent exactly the same discipline as all the other monks. When he was in training near his father at the Jetavana Monastery, a senior member of the Sangha returned from a long journey. Since rooms were assigned by seniority, Rahula had to give up his quarters to this monk. As luck would have it, it rained heavily the night he was forced to sleep outdoors, and he took refuge in a latrine. As might be expected, he grew very tired and dozed off. Suddenly he was awakened by a voice: "Who's there?" Recognizing it as his father's, Rahula identified himself. "I see," said Shakyamuni. After a moment's silence, Rahula heard the sound of his departing footsteps.

Though training at his father's side, Rahula was unable to call him father or draw close to him. Nor could he expect to receive from his father any sign of affection. Perhaps it was the sadness of being unable to treat his father as a father that prompted him to small acts of mischief. For instance, he once misdirected a lay believer who had come to the monastery and had asked him how to find Shakyamuni. Word of this reached Shakyamuni; that evening, to his son's great amazement, he took the unprecedented step of going to Rahula's quarters.

Rahula prepared his room and watched joyfully as his father approached. Inside the room, Shakyamuni called for water. Rahula brought it. When Rahula had washed his father's feet, Shakyamuni asked, "Rahula, can you drink this water?"

Rahula replied, "No. It was clean, but now that I have washed your feet in it, it's too dirty to drink."

Shakyamuni then instructed Rahula to throw the water away and return with the container. Rahula did as he was told, and Shakyamuni said, "Rahula, would you put food in this container?" Rahula answered, "No, I would not put food in a container that had just held dirty water."

Hearing this, Shakyamuni said, "A person who knows that lying is evil but lies anyway and hurts others is like water that is fouled or a container that has been dirtied. Sin begins with lying, which summons all evil to itself. And the suffering caused by lying inevitably rebounds upon the liar.''

Enlightened by Shakyamuni's words, from that time forth Rahula was diligent in quietly obeying all the rules of the Sangha and became revered among the other disciples as foremost in quietly doing good.

Many people looked on Rahula with sympathy. Though born and reared as the only son of a prince, he had given up his life of privilege at an early age to subject himself to a course of stern religious discipline. But within the Sangha some monks treated him with reserve, and some were jealous of him. Dealing with such attitudes was among his greatest ordeals.

Once, when Rahula and Sariputta were begging in Rajagaha, a hooligan threw sand in Sariputta's begging bowl and beat Rahula. Sariputta warned Rahula, "You are Shakyamuni's disciple. No matter what kind of treatment you encounter, you must never allow anger to enter your heart. You must always be compassionate to all beings. The bravest person, the person seeking enlightenment, abandons conceit and has the fortitude to resist anger." Rahula smiled and silently walked on till he came to a stream, where he washed the dirt from his body.

Rahula continued strict discipline of this kind until he attained enlightenment at the age of twenty. Later, after Shakyamuni allowed women into the Sangha, Rahula's mother, Yasodhara, became a nun and trained under Mahapajapati, Shakyamuni's aunt and foster mother, until she too attained enlightenment.

KACCHAYANA
Foremost in Explaining the Dharma

Kacchayana, foremost among the Buddha's disciples for his explanations of the Buddhist teachings, was born into a Brahman family in Ujjeni, the capital of Avanti, a kingdom far to the west of the places in northeastern India where Shakyamuni taught, such as the Bamboo Grove and Jetavana monasteries. Studious from childhood, he grew up in rivalry with his only brother, who was older than he.

Kacchayana's brother once left home to tour various regions and study literature and martial arts. After his return, he assembled the local people and expounded what he had learned. Soon Kacchayana too began gathering groups of people and instructing them with even greater skill than his brother. Unwilling to allow his brother to get the better of him, Kacchayana had studied assiduously during his absence. But his brother was equally unwilling to be outshone, and the rivalry between the two intensified until their father sent Kacchayana away to live with an uncle, the hermit-seer Asita, who lived on Mount Vindhya. This was the man who, on the birth of Prince Siddhattha, had predicted that if the child remained in the secular world he would become a "wheel-rolling king," or ideal ruler, and that if he abandoned the secular world for a life of religion he would become a buddha.

Asita willingly undertook the training of Kacchayana, whom he recognized as an intelligent boy. His efforts soon bore fruit, for Kacchayana is said to have immediately mastered the four stages of meditation and to have attained the five supernatural powers.

Asita firmly believed the day would come when an enlightened Prince Siddhattha would begin to expound the supreme teaching. But Asita was an old man and did not live to see it. Before his death, he told Kacchayana, "When the prince has attained enlightenment and has become a buddha, go to him and request that he teach you." Not long after Asita's death, word of Siddhattha's enlightenment reached Kacchayana. Imperceptibly, however, Kacchayana had grown proud of his own high level of meditation and supernatural powers. He forgot his uncle's bidding and lost the will to seek the Way. Instead, he became adept at inspiring people to make offerings to him.

Kacchayana's father was a councilor to Pajjota, the king of Avanti. When the king heard that Shakyamuni was expounding the supreme teaching in northeastern India, he became greatly interested. He instructed Kacchayana's father to send Kacchayana to the Buddha to see what kind of person he was and what philosophy he taught. In compliance with the king's orders, Kacchayana and seven ministers made the long journey to the Jetavana Monastery in Savatthi.

Though Kacchayana had considered his own state of training and discipline superior to all others', as soon as he met Shakyamuni he realized that here was a person who had attained a stage of development far beyond his own. It is said that he immediately asked to join the Sangha. Because Kacchayana had already advanced fairly far under Asita, he was able to understand everything Shakyamuni taught him and to explain it convincingly to others. This ability eventually earned him the epithet "foremost in explaining the Dharma." When he had mastered Shakyamuni's teachings, Kacchayana returned to Ujjeni to carry the Buddhist message to as many people as possible.

One day, as Kacchayana was approaching a river, he heard the sound of weeping. He stopped and, parting the tall grasses, saw an old woman crouching on the riverbank. He asked her in the gentlest possible voice, "What unhappiness makes you weep this way?" At first she stiffened in fear. But the kind eyes of the man gazing down on her eased her alarm, and haltingly she told her story.

She was a servant in the house of one of the wealthiest men in town. Though the man had several storehouses filled with riches, he was stingy and cruel. The woman said that every day was a living hell. Though old and weak, she was forced to work from dawn until late at night and was often whipped like a beast of burden. She was poorly fed. If she became too weary to move or did something wrong, she was beaten more severely. Lacking relatives or friends to protect her, she had no choice but to put up with this treatment. She was thinking of hanging herself. "Today I was told to come to the river to draw water, and I cried when I saw the reflection of my wretched face," she concluded.

As the old woman broke into tears again, Kacchayana said to her, "If you hate your poverty so much, why don't you sell it?"

Raising her face in amazement, the woman replied, "But no one buys poverty!"

"There is one person who buys it," said Kacchayana. "I will teach you about him. Do as I instruct you. First cleanse yourself in the river."

The old woman followed his instructions, though she looked doubtful.

"Now that you have cleansed yourself, you must make an offering."

"But I own nothing at all. Even this water jug belongs to my master," the woman answered.

"Yes, you do own something," Kacchayana said. "Go now and fill my begging bowl with pure water."

The woman did as she was told and gave the water to Kacchayana. Accepting her offering, he explained slowly and carefully, "Old woman, it is the Buddha who buys poverty. If you purify your heart as you cleansed your body with pure water, your soul will become an immense treasure. You could then give that treasure to others, just as you have given this water to me."

The old woman nodded, and Kacchayana continued, "Can you stop hating your master? Can you make up your mind to serve him well in all the work you undertake?"

Tears flowed from the old woman's eyes.

"Very well," said Kacchayana. "Tonight, after your master goes to sleep, meditate on the Buddha and remember that he is always by your side and that he understands your sufferings and hardships."

It is said that on the same night, in a corner of her master's house, the old woman died in tranquillity.

To convert people to Buddhism in a place so distant from where Shakyamuni himself was teaching must have demanded tremendous effort. Kacchayana meditated upon and organized the teachings he had received from Shakyamuni so that he could explain the Dharma convincingly to others.

Once, when Kacchayana was resting with a group of people beside a pond, an old Brahman, leaning on a stick, joined the assembly and stood for a while observing. Then he tottered toward Kacchayana and angrily asked if none of the people in the gathering knew the respect due the elderly. Kacchayana said quietly that he had never forgotten the reverence due to age but that he saw no elderly people around him.

"I am older than all the rest of you," snapped the Brahman, "yet no one showed me proper courtesy when I came to this place!"

Kacchayana remained calm as he said, "Shakyamuni teaches that though a person is eighty or ninety years old, white haired and toothless, if he is still obsessed with the desires of the five senses—sight, hearing, smell, taste, and touch—he is a child. And a person who is twenty-five, with lustrous skin and black hair, is an elder if he has been liberated from the desires of affectionate attachment." Hearing this, the old Brahman was abashed and departed in silence.

Although Shakyamuni never went to Avanti, Kacchayana continued to be devoted to him. And Shakyamuni never forgot his disciple Kacchayana, who was spreading the Buddhist teachings in a distant land. Later, when a man named Sona, who had accepted the Buddhist faith because of Kacchayana's teaching, made the long and difficult journey to the Jetavana Monastery to hear Shakyamuni directly, he described to Shakyamuni in detail the valuable work Kacchayana was doing in Avanti.

SUBHUTI
Foremost in Understanding the Doctrine of the Void

My hut is well roofed. No wind can enter, and it is comfortable. Gods, make it rain as hard as you like. My mind, making diligence its abode, is wholly tranquil and liberated. Gods, make it rain as hard as you like." This passage in the *Theragatha* is attributed to Subhuti, who was revered as foremost among the Buddha's disciples in nonbelligerence and in understanding of the doctrine of the Void, the teaching that there is no fixed, permanent self.

The above passage is said to have been composed to mark the presentation of a house to Subhuti by King Bimbisara of Magadha. Though the day of the presentation ceremony drew near, the carpenter had still not thatched the roof. The king prayed that it would not rain until the building was finished, but this alarmed the peasants, who were afraid their crops would wither. Sympathetic to the peasants, Subhuti is said to have recited this prayer for rain, which he had no need to fear, since diligence was the true abode of his mind.

Before becoming one of Shakyamuni's disciples, Subhuti had been a man plagued by anger. Once he had freed himself from that emotion, however, he was able to remain calm even at the thought of being drenched by rain pouring through the roof of his house. He was able to say, "My true abode is the secure house of the knowledge that all things in the universe are insubstantial, homogeneous, and equal. Thus I am at ease no matter what the weather. Therefore, gods, for the sake of the peasants and their crops, let it rain." His verse overflows with the joy of freedom from attachment to transient phenomena that understanding of the doctrine of the Void brings.

Subhuti was the son of Sumana, who was the younger brother of Sudatta, the wealthy merchant who donated the Jetavana Monastery to Shakyamuni. As a child Subhuti was so attractive and intelligent that his parents had high hopes for him and took great care in his upbringing. But as he grew older, people came to dislike him. Even neighbors who had formerly been friendly would frown at the very sight of him. This was due to his habit of speaking ill of everyone he encountered.

After a while his anger was directed not only at human beings but at other creatures, as well. He even hurled stones and curses at birds in the sky. His parents and relatives could do nothing to control his raging. After a series of quarrels with his mother and father, one day a reprimand of theirs caused Subhuti to run away from home. He dashed into the nearby mountains and refused to return.

But the quiet of the forest and mountains did not calm his anger. Stamping on the ground and throwing stones at birds, he moved deeper and deeper into the woods. Suddenly he was surprised by the abrupt appearance of an old man, who asked gently, "Why have you come alone into this forest?"

Subhuti retorted brusquely, "Everyone makes a fool of me. Today my father scolded me and made me so angry that I ran away from home."

Remaining calm in the face of Subhuti's curtness, the old man said, "Being angry without doing good will only increase your suffering. It cannot benefit you in any way. At the Jetavana Monastery, near Savatthi, there is a noble man who teaches human beings how to abandon evil and do good. You should go to him and ask to be allowed to hear his teaching."

Subhuti had become tired of the vicious circle of being shunned by others because of his angry outbursts and then of taking their attitude as cause for further irritation. He decided to follow the old man's advice. The knowledge that the Jetavana Monastery had been built by his uncle Sudatta may also have influenced his decision.

That morning Savatthi bustled with people. This was the day on which the Jetavana Monastery, donated by Sudatta as a place where the Buddhist teachings could be expounded, was to be presented to Shakyamuni.

Subhuti entered the building with a group eager to hear the Buddha's teaching. When he beheld Shakyamuni's radiant countenance and welcoming smile, Subhuti felt the mass of discontent that had built up within him dissipate. He made up his mind then and there to request acceptance as one of the Buddha's disciples.

After the presentation ceremony he approached Shakyamuni and asked to be admitted to the Sangha.

Shakyamuni gazed at Subhuti and said, "Short temper is clearly written on your face. There is no room for irritability in the discipline of a monk's life. You must have patience and forbearance. Do you think you can develop these traits?"

Subhuti was silent. Shakyamuni continued, "If you are constantly angry, without trying to alter your mental attitude, evil will increase day by day until finally the very seeds of goodness will disappear. An irascible man's anger makes him suffer the torments of hell, since he is constantly poisoning his own mind with a venom that leads to faultfinding and killing. He shuts himself up in his own suffering until ultimately he is unable to find a way out of it."

Through Shakyamuni's words, Subhuti came to see clearly the cause of his own ceaseless suffering. His constantly finding fault with others had robbed him of the flexibility necessary for peace of mind, and he had been continually hounded by the fear that the people he had abused would attack him in retaliation. The thought of the retribution he would have to suffer for the countless sins he had committed in his rage terrified Subhuti, and he repented profoundly of the harm he had done not only to people but also to animals and birds.

After Subhuti had become a disciple, Shakyamuni taught him, "The attitude of blaming others arises from the idea that others exist because one exists oneself and from the self-centered notion that all others are mistaken." Subhuti was also taught that the way to eliminate the effects of his past sins was to assimilate thoroughly the doctrine of causal origination and thus to realize that his own existence depended on the existence of others.

"It is wrong to be obsessed by desires and to yearn for pleasure," Shakyamuni told him. "It is also wrong to find the source of desires in one's own physical being and consequently torment one's body. The follower of the Way avoids both extremes.

"The follower of the Way does not speak of others behind their back, since doing so leads to falsehood. The follower of the Way does not speak rapidly: though the fast talker understands his own meaning, others may misunderstand.

"The follower of the Way does not speak in his own local tongue. The same vessel is called by different names in different regions, and it may be taken for its very opposite. Thinking that only what one says oneself is correct invites misunderstanding on the part of others.

"Failure to keep these teachings arises from attachment to one's own being. And this is the origin of all conflict."

For the rest of his life, Subhuti abided by these teachings and never again became angry no matter how much he was persecuted. Severing all attachment to his own being, he achieved a state of selflessness and was revered as the disciple who understood the doctrine of the Void better than all others.

Without faith, the difficult task of attaining selflessness is impossible. At one point, after paying reverence to Shakyamuni, Subhuti asked him, "Revered teacher, what is the nature of faith? What should a person do to become ardently faithful?"

Shakyamuni replied, "Revere and keep the precepts. Hear, understand, and follow the Dharma. Establish good relations with your fellow monks in the Sangha. Be submissive when exhorted, be diligent in discipline, and be joyful in carrying out the teachings."

Although he was inconspicuous among the Buddha's ten great disciples, Subhuti loved and respected his master and, thoroughly disciplining himself in the teaching that his own existence depended on the existence of others, ultimately attained enlightenment.

PUNNA-MANTANIPUTTA
Foremost in Teaching the Dharma

As the rainy season approached, Shakyamuni's disciples returned to their home districts to reflect quietly on what they had heard and done in the previous season, to repent of shortcomings, to be diligent in meditation, and to renew their will to attain enlightenment. After the rainy season, when they returned to their master, he looked fondly at each and then said, "You all look well and seem to have made excellent use of your retreat. I think all of you have advanced through discipline and training. Still, there is something I should like to ask of you.

"Is there anyone among you who is esteemed for the following qualities by those who devotedly pursue the same course of discipline? Is there anyone among you who lives wanting little and knowing that little is enough and who praises lack of desire and realization of sufficiency as wonderful and precious? Is there anyone among you who diligently strives in solitude and praises the accomplishment of not being misled either by solitude or worldliness, saying that such an accomplishment is wonderful and precious? Is there anyone among you who strives and extols the wonder and value of striving? Is there anyone among you who, observing the precepts, being diligent in meditation, and having attained wisdom, praises the value and magnificence of the precepts, meditation, and wisdom? Is there anyone among you who, having attained the liberation of enlightenment and the Eye of Wisdom, praises the wonder and value of enlightenment and the attainment of the Eye of Wisdom through it? Is there anyone among you whose words and acts agree so splendidly that they encourage his fellow monks, awaken in them the desire to pursue the Way, and give them joy?"

The monks replied in unison, "World-honored One, there is one person of the kind you describe. He is none other than Punna-Mantaniputta."

On hearing this, Sariputta, who was sitting beside Shakyamuni, thought that Punna must be a wonderful and happy man if his fellow monks were in such agreement about him before their teacher.

Eventually Sariputta met Punna. Punna's speech was so lucid and cogent, each word so well chosen, that Sariputta imagined he was hearing Shakyamuni speak. He realized that none of Shakyamuni's other disciples could expound the master's teachings as correctly. Sariputta praised Punna, saying that a disciple like him was a source of supreme joy to all who heard him teach. Punna, in return, praised Sariputta's discourse.

Punna's eloquence made him known as foremost in teaching the Dharma. But he had not always been such a fine person. His father was a wealthy landed Brahman in the village of Donavatthu, in the kingdom of Kosala. His mother, Mantani, was the younger sister of Kondanna, one of Shakyamuni's earliest disciples. Mantani reared Punna with the greatest care and affection.

Blessed with superior qualities and a fine environment, Punna grew into a brilliant youth. But everyone has faults, and Punna's greatest fault was pride, probably because he had been so indulged. Even marriage to a beautiful woman who made him the envy of all did not satisfy him. When he realized that people praised his mother and wife but not him, he became jealous and wondered why this should be, since he was so much more outstanding. His jealousy kept him constantly on edge. Finally one day he realized that praising his mother and wife was the same as praising him. He felt ashamed of the conceit that had made him angry when people failed to praise him.

Overwhelmed by his shortcomings, Punna decided to make a fresh start. Leaving home, wife, and children, for the next twenty years he devoted himself completely to Brahman discipline. He achieved great success and attracted a large following.

Punna firmly believed in the correctness of his own philosophy. When he heard that Shakyamuni was teaching in Rajagaha, he immediately went there with twenty-nine disciples to challenge him to a debate, confident that he, Punna, would win. Shakyamuni greeted Punna quietly and persuaded him of the futility of debate, explaining that instead of engaging in debate people should seek liberation through dialogue.

Punna realized the importance of Shakyamuni's teachings and asked Shakyamuni to accept him as a disciple. His followers did the same. The solemnity of their ordination deeply moved all the beholders.

OTHER DISCIPLES

DABBA
The Servant of the Sangha

The *Theragatha* contains the following passage ascribed to a monk named Dabba-Mallaputta: "Dabba, who was hard to tame but is now tamed by self-taming, is content, with doubts overcome; victorious, with fears truly gone; because Dabba has attained perfect tranquillity."

Dabba was a monk who voluntarily undertook to perform the various services needed by the other members of the Sangha. He cleaned their rooms, prepared their bedding, and served their meals. Often he was the victim of misunderstanding, resentment, and even false accusations by the other monks. Dabba is said to have recited the words quoted above after one such misunderstanding was resolved.

Dabba was born into a princely family in the kingdom of Malla, near the Shakya domain, where Shakyamuni was born. When Dabba was seven, Shakyamuni went to Malla to preach. Dabba's grandmother, a deeply religious woman who had reared the boy ever since his mother's death shortly after he was born, took him to hear the Buddha.

Shakyamuni seemed a splendid person to the young

boy. Dabba felt as if he were enfolded in a gentle radiance emanating from the Buddha. He felt as calm and safe as if his mother held him in her arms once again.

"The Buddha is the most noble of men," his grandmother told him. "He left his home, gave up his princely rank, devoted himself to religious practice, and finally attained enlightenment in order to save those who suffer in this earthly life."

Her words made a strong impression on Dabba. "I want to become like him. I'd like to follow him," he thought. Perhaps because he had lost his mother so early, Dabba found that his desire to be with the Buddha grew stronger day by day and year by year. Finally, at the age of fourteen, with his family's consent, he was admitted into the Sangha as a novice. He plunged into religious training and by the age of sixteen had reached a deep understanding of the Four Noble Truths and the Eightfold Path, approaching the state of an *arahant,* one free from all cravings and no longer subject to rebirth.

When Dabba received the "perfect precepts" of the fully ordained monk at the age of twenty, he made a decision. He felt fortunate to have heard the Buddha's teachings and to have studied the profound truth of the Dharma while still young. But to enter fully into the realm of truth and completely destroy the illusion of self, he decided to undertake further severe discipline. He would pay reverence to all the monks and perform the various tasks necessary to the daily life of the Sangha. This would be his religious practice. After Dabba received the Buddha's approval of his plan, he renewed his resolve to serve the other monks without selfishness or partiality.

In preparing the monks' rooms, he spared no effort to see that their days of meditation were undisturbed. He allocated the rooms so that monks who practiced the formal recitation of the teachings could all be together; and the same for those who devoted themselves to keeping the precepts with special strictness, and for those who made preaching the Dharma their personal practice. He made sure that every monk's needs were seen to: there were rooms set aside for those who were physically weak, and there was appropriate bedding for the elderly. If a wandering monk appeared at the monastery late at night, Dabba would leave his bed and carefully show the newcomer where things were: bedding, pillows, water for drinking and for washing, and so on. Thus he devoted himself completely to the service of the monastic community.

The most difficult task of all was the fair division of food among the monks. Dabba made a point of remembering which of the monks needed more food and which needed less when he distributed the food offered by pious lay people or collected by the monks during their daily begging rounds.

One day a monk named Laludayi approached Dabba as he distributed the food and challenged him: "What gives you the right to be the only one to divide up our food? Lately I've been getting nothing but scraps. You're unfair! *I'll* do the dividing up from now on."

When the Sangha agreed to Laludayi's demand, Dabba was crushed. He felt that the others did not appreciate his efforts to distribute the food fairly. Laludayi was a member of the Sangha and was supposed to have abandoned worldly desires and pleasures. Yet he had complained loudly about unfairness, comparing his portion with his neighbors'. Dabba wondered why Laludayi had entered the religious life in the first place.

Two or three days after Laludayi had begun to divide up the food, the situation was clearly out of hand. The monks quickly realized how truly fair Dabba's method of division had been, and Dabba renewed his resolve, thinking, "It is precisely because this kind of work is disagreeable and goes unappreciated that it can serve as an excellent practice for me." The other monks soon asked him deferentially to return to his former duties.

Some years passed, and one day a wealthy lay believer from Rajagaha visited the Bamboo Grove Monastery. Listening to Dabba's preaching, he was moved to say, "Your words have aroused in me a deep desire to acquire merit so as to be reborn in heaven. I hope some of the members of the venerable Sangha will honor me by coming to my home tomorrow to receive the offerings of food that I shall prepare."

After Dabba had accepted his invitation, the lay believer asked which of the monks would be sent to his house. When he was told that Mettiya and Bhummajaka would go, his face fell. These two monks, who were brothers, were infamous for their rudeness and arrogance, a reputation that had spread even among the laity. But a lay believer was not permitted to choose the monks to whom he would make offerings, so he could only acquiesce.

When he returned home, the layman angrily gave orders to his maidservant: "We're going to have to make offerings to those worthless monks Mettiya and Bhummajaka. When they arrive tomorrow, show them to the granary and give them the worst food we have."

Mettiya and Bhummajaka had no idea of the cold

welcome awaiting them, of course. They were so over-joyed at the thought of the wonderful cuisine the rich man would be preparing for them that they were up at the crack of dawn with their robes and bowls in readiness, and off they went to the layman's mansion in Rajagaha. To their surprise, a mere maidservant greeted them. And when they were led to the gloomy granary and saw the coarse food that was set before them, they became angry, saying they had come at the invitation of the master of the house and demanding to know where he was.

"The master is away on urgent business, but he left instructions for me to entertain you, reverend sirs," said the maidservant.

"To entertain us?" asked Mettiya. "In this granary? With this kind of food?"

"Yes, sir. It is all just as the master ordered."

"Idiot! He thinks we're going to accept these offer-ings!" Mettiya shouted angrily. Kicking over the low tables set before them, Mettiya and Bhummajaka left hurriedly for the Bamboo Grove Monastery. Mettiya, who was literally trembling with rage, said, "This is all Dabba's doing! We stood up to him, and so to pay us back he devised this scheme to shame us by getting the layman to issue a bogus invitation!"

Just then a nun happened by and Mettiya hit upon a plan. Putting on a smile, he addressed the nun po-litely: "Reverend sister. You know the senior monk Dabba? He has the appearance of virtue but in fact constantly insults and mistreats the two of us out of spite. Today, for example, he and a lay believer con-spired to bring great shame on my brother and me. But there is a limit even to our patience. We have to do *something*—don't you agree?"

"Indeed, it is very wrong of Dabba to do such things."

"Yes, and to continue to allow such a biased man to be part of the Sangha is to bring shame on us all. So we would like you, reverend sister, to go to the Buddha and tell him that Dabba has made improper advances to you and thus broken the precept against sexual misconduct. This is necessary to preserve the purity of the Sangha."

The simple nun agreed and, presenting herself before the Buddha, repeated what she had been told to say. Then the Buddha summoned Dabba before the assembled members of the Sangha and questioned him: "Dabba, you have been accused of breaking the precept against sexual misconduct. Have you ever done such a thing?"

Dabba looked steadily at the Buddha and replied, "The World-honored One knows far better than anyone else whether I would break such a precept."

But the Buddha repeated his question: "Dabba, have you ever broken the precept against sexual misconduct?"

"World-honored One, it is as you know it to be," Dabba replied. Inwardly, he was deeply hurt, thinking, "Does the Buddha really believe the words of Mettiya and Bhummajaka? Does he think me the kind of monk who would engage in immorality? Have all my efforts in religious practice gone unnoticed? Were they all in vain?"

Dabba was aroused from his thoughts by the Buddha's strong, insistent voice: "Dabba, you must state clearly before the Sangha whether or not you have broken the precept against immorality!" At that moment Dabba experienced a kind of awakening. His self-concern, his need to defend himself—this was precisely the greatest obstacle to full liberation!

"World-honored One, this accusation is baseless." As he spoke, he felt as if dark clouds were lifting from his heart. Dabba's statement was accepted as true by the Buddha and the Sangha. Then Mettiya and Bhummajaka were called forward. They could hide nothing from the Buddha's penetrating insight; and thus Dabba's name was cleared.

This experience taught Dabba to see things in a new light. Until then he had always secretly hoped that the other members of the Sangha would show appreciation for his hard work at such lowly tasks. But this attitude itself was a kind of selfish attachment. And the more effort he made to serve the monks, the stronger this particular attachment grew. To destroy it, he decided to devote himself with even greater energy and purity of intention to serving the Sangha.

Soon it began to be rumored that a radiance could be seen flowing from Dabba's fingertips as he guided visiting monks about the monastery at night. There were even some monks who made a point of visiting the monastery after dark in order to observe the mysterious light. Dabba would guide them cheerfully, walking through the dark monastery grounds without hesitation. And indeed, the monks following him could see his fingertips glowing with a strange radiance.

Thus Dabba-Mallaputta, by devoting himself totally to serving the Sangha, received the veneration and gratitude of all his fellow monks and was able to attain enlightenment of a high order.

AMBAPALI
The Courtesan Who Became a Nun

To the north of Rajagaha, the capital of Magadha, was the city of Vesali, the capital of the Vajji confederation, which ranked with Magadha in power. As a baby, Ambapali had been abandoned under a tree in a garden outside the city of Vesali. Her parentage was unknown. The gardener who discovered her named her Ambapali, meaning "she who was born beneath the *amba* [mango] tree." The child grew into an extraordinarily beautiful woman, with glowing skin, long black hair, and large eyes. Her beauty became famous throughout the region, and an endless stream of young men, both from the city and from far away, came to seek her hand in marriage. Princes and rich men's sons vied with one another for her favor. The elders of Vesali, concerned that fighting would break out among Ambapali's many suitors, decided to make her a city courtesan and thus satisfy everyone, as well as make money for the city.

Courtesans were beautiful and accomplished women who entertained their customers with a variety of skills. They were important to the economy of Vesali, where men of many lands gathered to trade. Housed in

fine mansions, they lived lives of luxury. Soon people
everywhere knew of Ambapali the courtesan, beautiful, charming, and clever. Drawn by her reputation,
many came to see her: citizens of Vesali, of course,
but also princes and rich men from surrounding
kingdoms. Stunned by a beauty and charm surpass-
ing their expectations, they poured out their wealth
to win her heart.

The number of rich men who chose to come to
Vesali to trade grew by the day, and soon Ambapali
was living in a splendid mansion, surrounded by servants who saw to her every need. She also acquired a
large orchard just outside the city. And yet Ambapali
found herself prey to anxiety. "The noblemen are in
love with my beauty, and the rich gladly give me their
treasures. Why, then, am I so uneasy?" she wondered.
Pondering the reason, she realized that it stemmed
from a deep fear that she would someday lose her
charms: "It's for my beauty that people love me and
give me these treasures, but one day that beauty will
be gone."

Soon after Ambapali began to be tormented by
thoughts like these, she learned that Shakyamuni had
come with his disciples from Magadha on his way
north and was staying in her orchard outside Vesali.
Some years earlier there had been an epidemic in the
city. Shakyamuni and his disciples, who had been
visiting the city at the time, had devoted themselves
to caring for the sick. As a result of their efforts many
had been saved, and since then the people of Vesali
had been devout followers of Shakyamuni.

Hearing that Shakyamuni had come, people rushed
to the orchard. Ambapali, too, having bathed and
purified her body, hurriedly set out with her servants,

riding in a carriage decorated with gold fittings and fresh flowers. She arrived as Shakyamuni was preaching: "Everything in this world is unstable and impermanent, yet people constantly try to hold on to other people and to things. It is because of this attachment that sorrow arises. To gain release from such sorrow, one should perform works of charity and observe the precepts. Thus one may obtain a favorable rebirth in the heavens."

Ambapali trembled as she heard Shakyamuni explain the necessity of making offerings to gain release from the desire to grasp things that are by nature impermanent. Imbued with new hope, she wished she could be with Shakyamuni forever. Reverently she approached him and asked, "World-honored One, I am Ambapali the courtesan. Will you deign to grant the request of a lowly woman like me? I would be honored if you would visit my home tomorrow morning and allow me to present offerings of food to you and your disciples. I am eager to hear more of your profound teachings." Ambapali was filled with awe as she spoke, but Shakyamuni smiled gently and agreed to her request.

Ambapali was overjoyed at the thought that the Buddha had accepted an invitation from someone like her. She left at once to prepare the food, urging her driver to hurry. When they had gone halfway, they came upon several richly decorated carriages approaching from the opposite direction. The local princes, having heard of Shakyamuni's visit, were hurrying to the orchard hoping to catch a glimpse of him, while Ambapali and her retinue were rushing home to prepare offerings for the following morning. The two groups collided in the middle of the road.

The princes leaped from their carriages and surrounded Ambapali's, accusing her of causing the accident and demanding payment for the damage done. But when they realized that the beautiful woman who stood before them apologizing so politely was the courtesan Ambapali, they calmed down and spoke more temperately. Ambapali explained that the reason she was in such a hurry was that Shakyamuni had agreed to accept offerings of food at her home the following morning. She wanted to reach home as quickly as possible and begin preparations for his visit.

At this news the princes again became very excited. One said, "What! You mean it's already been decided that Shakyamuni will breakfast at your house tomorrow? That won't do! We had planned to invite Shakyamuni to accept *our* offerings tomorrow morning. That's why we're hurrying to the orchard. Ambapali, there's no need for you to pay for the damage to our carriages, but we'd like you to let us entertain Shakyamuni tomorrow in your stead."

"Oh, no! I'm very sorry to have to refuse your request, but I just cannot agree."

The princes would not give up, however, and pressed her even harder. One said, "Ambapali, let us entertain the Buddha and we will give you a thousand pieces of gold. No, wait! We will give you half our fortunes if only you will agree." The princes were sure a courtesan would give in if only she were offered enough money.

But Ambapali flatly refused. "No. Even if you offered me all the treasures in this city, I could not agree to your request." She said this because she knew that the doctrine Shakyamuni taught was uniquely precious, and that nothing in the world was more important than to follow his teachings and acquire merit by making offerings to the Buddha and the Sangha.

Thus Ambapali resisted the princes' inducements and entertained the Buddha and his disciples the next morning. After receiving the offerings, the Buddha explained to her how suffering arises and how it can be destroyed. Listening to him, Ambapali realized how mistaken her way of life was—taking pride in her physical beauty and relying on the acquisition of worldly wealth to bring happiness. Vowing to revere the Three Treasures of the Buddha, the Dharma, and the Sangha, to observe the precepts, and to lead a virtuous life, Ambapali offered her orchard to the Buddha and the Sangha as a retreat. Then she was instructed to keep the five precepts of the lay Buddhist: not to take life, not to steal, not to indulge in sexual misconduct, not to lie, and not to drink intoxicants.

Soon thereafter Ambapali asked to be admitted to the Sangha. The rest of her life was devoted to the difficult search for true enlightenment under the Buddha's guidance. As a nun she composed the following passage, recorded in the *Therigatha,* expressing her understanding of the Buddha's teaching in relation to her own earlier experience as a courtesan:

"Once my hair was beautiful, adorned with gold, fragrant and soft, well plaited. Now, because of old age, it has fallen out. There is no error in the words of the speaker of truth. . . .

"Once my eyes were dark blue and long, shining brilliantly like jewels. Now, because of old age, they have lost their luster. There is no error in the words of the speaker of truth. . . .

"Once my teeth were beautiful, the color of the buds

of the plantain. Now, because of old age, they are broken and yellowish, like grains of wheat. There is no error in the words of the speaker of truth.

"Once my voice was sweet, like that of a cuckoo flying around in the forest. Now, because of old age, it falters. There is no error in the words of the speaker of truth. . . .

"Once my body was beautiful, like a burnished sheet of gold. Now, because of old age, it is covered with fine wrinkles. There is no error in the words of the speaker of truth. . . .

"Thus this body, an aggregate of elements, has grown old and is the abode of many sufferings. It is a decayed house whose plaster has fallen off. There is no error in the words of the speaker of truth."

GENERAL SIHA
The Challenger of the Buddha

Vesali, the capital of the Vajji confederation, was one of the greatest cities of India in Shakyamuni's time, a commercial center on a par with Rajagaha and Savatthi. Shakyamuni began visiting Vesali to preach soon after attaining enlightenment. Many townspeople were converted to Buddhism, and they built a monastery called the Gabled Hall in a forest outside the city. At the time of this story, Shakyamuni was staying there.

The nobles of the Vajji confederation were holding a meeting in the public hall of Vesali. The hall was crowded with representatives from all over the land. During the discussion of public affairs, someone mentioned the holy man Shakyamuni, whereupon many in the assembly began praising him and his teachings.

"The Buddha, the Dharma he teaches, and his Sangha are truly wonderful. He must be an enlightened sage."

"Even the king of neighboring Magadha has become a follower of Shakyamuni."

One man sat silently, listening attentively to all that was said. This impressive figure was General Siha, famous throughout the Vajji confederation, and a pious follower of the Jain faith for many years. There were many supporters of Jainism in the area; in fact, the founder of the religion, Nigantha-Nataputta, was a scion of the royal house of Vajji.

General Siha, hearing Shakyamuni so highly praised by so many, was eager to meet him, for he was curious about just what Shakyamuni taught. That very day, on his way home, General Siha went to visit Nigantha-Nataputta, his religious master. "Reverend sir," he said, "the fame of the holy man Shakyamuni is very great. I should like to visit him and hear his teaching." General Siha said this hoping to be able to refute Shakyamuni. But the Jain master coldly forbade a visit to Shakyamuni, saying, "General Siha, Shakyamuni is nothing but an advocate of inaction who denies the possibility of free will or self-determined action of any kind. What need is there for you, a follower of the orthodox Jain teachings, to listen to such false doctrines?" General Siha, having been rebuked by his teacher, had no choice but to abandon his plan to meet Shakyamuni.

At the next assembly, again the holy man Shakyamuni's praises were on everyone's lips; and when the same thing happened at the following assembly, as well, General Siha was no longer able to suppress his curiosity. He hurried home and set out, accompanied by many attendants, to visit the Buddha, who was preaching at the Gabled Hall.

As General Siha listened to the Buddha, he was overcome with such emotion that his body trembled. The Buddha's countenance was gentle and noble, and his body seemed surrounded by a spiritual radiance. He noticed General Siha standing at a distance, gazing at him steadily. The Buddha smiled and beckoned General Siha to a seat near him. The general bowed reverently.

"General Siha, do you have something you wish to say to me, or some question you wish to ask?"

General Siha looked intently at the Buddha and said, "I have been told by teachers of other religions that the holy man Shakyamuni is one who preaches inaction, saying that people are pawns of fate and are incapable of free, self-determined action. Or that you are an annihilationist, who teaches that nothing remains after death; or that you are one who teaches hatred of this world. Are these statements true, or are they just slander?"

The Buddha replied gently, "General Siha, I do not know in what sense these statements by other teachers should be understood. If they are to be taken in the following sense, then I agree with them. I teach the avoidance of evil in thought, word, and deed. In that sense I am indeed an advocate of inaction. Furthermore, I teach that evil actions can be annihilated by destroying the roots of greed, anger, and ignorance within people's hearts. To that extent I may be said to be an annihilationist. And finally, I do indeed abhor all evil actions, and in that sense I may be said to hate the world."

General Siha was deeply impressed by the skill of the Buddha's reply. Without so much as a word of direct criticism of other religious teachers, he managed to use their ill-intentioned remarks to expound his own teaching.

"This is an extraordinary man," thought General Siha as he put another question: "Some religious teachers say that you are an extreme ascetic who

teaches the mortification of the body; others say you
are a quietist, approving of the quest for consolation.
Are either of these evaluations correct?"

"General Siha, I am one who ceaselessly practices
discipline in order to cut the roots of evil in thought,
word, and deed. In that sense I am an ascetic. And I advocate such ceaseless practice in order that people may
be led to the realm of perfect peace. In that sense I
preach the quest for consolation."

As he listened to the Buddha reply so calmly and
reasonably, a feeling of absolute trust arose in General
Siha. He thought, "The holy man Shakyamuni is indeed one who has perceived the truth. He is surely a
buddha, who through the power of wisdom and compassion changes all that is defiled into purity and all
evil karma into good." Full of joy, he bowed reverently and earnestly addressed the Buddha again:
"World-honored One, you have shown the true
Dharma to me, a follower of another path, like raising a fallen tree or showing the way to a man who is
lost. You are the supreme sage, the Buddha. Please
allow me to become your follower, to take refuge in
the Buddha, the Dharma, and the Sangha."

To his surprise, however, the Buddha refused his request. "General Siha, you are an eminent leader in
this land. You are a well-known, high-ranking sup-
porter of the Jain faith. It would be best for you to consider well before you become my follower."

General Siha could hardly believe his ears. When he
had become a Jain, the monks of that order had gone
through the streets with raised banners announcing
the conversion of so influential and noble a man. Yet
the Buddha urged him to reflect carefully before he
became a Buddhist. Deeply moved, he thought, "The

Buddha does not consider the possible profit to his own order; he thinks only of the salvation of his hearer. He seeks only the spread of the true Dharma."

Again General Siha bowed low before the Buddha and repeated his request: "Your words have only served to confirm my faith, World-honored One. I wish to take refuge in the Three Treasures. I shall not deviate from this resolve as long as I live. Please accept me as a lay disciple."

But still the Buddha would not agree. "General Siha, for many years you have generously supported the Jain monks; you must not now cease giving them offerings. You have great influence, so before you think of entering a new path, you must consider carefully the effect your acts will have on those who depend on you."

General Siha was abashed at these words. The Jain monks had been slandering the Buddha, saying that he taught that only those who made offerings to the Buddhist Sangha would gain merit and that there was no merit in supporting the monks of other paths. In fact, though, far from working only for the benefit of his own order, the Buddha had told General Siha that he should continue to support the Jain monks even if he became a Buddhist. What could better exemplify the spirit of charity, of true religion and virtue?

Firm in his resolve, for the third time he paid reverence to the Buddha and spoke: "Hearing the Buddha's words, my faith is as firm as a rock. Now, for the third time, I take refuge in the Three Treasures and vow to continue the good work of making offerings to the Jain monks as long as I live. Please accept me as a lay disciple."

Having been accepted, General Siha at once asked to

be allowed to make offerings of food, and the Buddha agreed to this request. Early the following morning General Siha and his servants welcomed Shakyamuni and his disciples and led them to a hall where places had been set and the finest foods laid out. When the meal was over and the Buddha was about to preach, General Siha called together all the members of his household and asked the Buddha about the merits of making offerings.

The Buddha responded, "Those who give generously to people in need obtain the following four practical benefits. First, they will be loved and respected by many because of their generosity. Second, they will be loved by people of excellence because of their generosity. Third, they will be praised by others for their generosity. Fourth, they will feel neither fear nor shame toward others on account of their generosity. In addition to these four practical benefits, General Siha, there is also the future benefit of being reborn in the heavenly realms after death as a reward for generosity in this life."

General Siha listened attentively to the Buddha's words and then said, "I knew of the four practical benefits attached to the practice of making offerings, but I had never learned of a future benefit. You have told us that one who gives generously will be reborn in the heavenly realms. Starting this very day, I shall, with complete faith in what the Buddha preaches, practice as you instruct me."

The Buddha then taught General Siha and his household the Four Noble Truths and the Eightfold Path. The general and his household, encountering the Buddhist teaching for the first time, were filled with joy. General Siha's daughter-in-law Yasomati made a request of the general: "Father, I too would like to perform a meritorious deed. Is there not some way for me to do so?" The general knew that Yasomati was a talented and virtuous young woman, so he invited the Buddha and his disciples to breakfast again the next morning, this time in her name. After hearing the Buddha preach again, she conceived a strong desire for enlightenment and determined to give generously to the Sangha from then on.

General Siha's niece, also named Siha, was so deeply moved that she asked her uncle's permission to enter the Sangha as a nun. The general agreed, and the Buddha admitted her. According to the *Therigatha,* Siha devoted herself to the exacting practice of meditation for a full seven years but was unable to attain enlightenment because of the strength of her remaining worldly attachments. Despairing, she went alone deep into the forest, tied a rope to a tree branch, and prepared to hang herself. At that very moment her delusions fell away and she attained enlightenment. She lived a long life and was revered by all as an accomplished nun.

So it happened that General Siha and his household, once fervent Jains, became devout Buddhists. After his conversion General Siha continued to perform works of charity and was held in the highest regard by the Vajji people.

SUJATA
The First Female Lay Disciple

Sujata, a beautiful and charming young woman, was the daughter of a prosperous farmer in Senani, a hamlet in the village of Uruvela, situated on the upper reaches of the Neranjara River southwest of Rajagaha, the capital of Magadha. Each morning Sujata would go to the pastures with her father's farmhands. Surrounded by the beauty of nature, yet quite unaware of her own beauty, Sujata happily went about her daily tasks.

On the banks of the Neranjara River, on the edge of the hamlet, there was a great *nigrodha* tree worshiped as the dwelling place of a god. Every morning and evening Sujata visited the tree to pray for a fine husband. The tree god heard the young woman's prayer, and soon a request for Sujata's hand came from the head of the richest family in Senani. Decked with flowers and jewels, she was married in great state amid general rejoicing. When the feasting and revelry were over, she went at once to the *nigrodha* tree and offered a prayer of thanksgiving to the god. Then she added a further petition: "Holy One, please protect my new family, and give me a fine, healthy baby boy to be its heir." Very soon she found herself with child and in due course gave birth to a jewellike baby boy. Sujata's heart was filled with happiness. She worshiped the tree god with even greater fervor and served her husband and other family members diligently, thankful for her good fortune.

Each year on the night of the full moon of Vesakha, the fifth month of the lunar calendar, Sujata prepared milk gruel to offer to the tree god. She used all her skill in preparing the gruel, which was always rich, thick, and delicious. Six years passed like a dream following her marriage to the richest man in Senani, and once again it was the night of the full moon of Vesakha. The silver rays of the moon covered the pastures and forests and transformed the Neranjara River into a flood of light. Sujata got up long before dawn and, together with Punna, her maid, whom she loved like a younger sister, began to milk the prize cows.

The two women poured the fresh milk, which seemed especially rich this time, into a pot in the kitchen, added rice, and began to boil the mixture. Soon a wonderful fragrance filled the kitchen. Sujata, busy feeding the fire with brushwood, felt a strange premonition. Usually she had to cope with smoke billowing up from the firewood and with milk suddenly boiling over; but this time not a single drop of the gruel was wasted, and the brushwood burned without giving off any smoke. As she stood watching and wondering, the milk gruel was finished—the best she had ever made! She instructed Punna to hurry and purify the altar at the foot of the *nigrodha* tree so that they could make the offering right away.

The full moon had moved to the west, and the eastern sky was growing lighter. Punna scurried through the predawn dimness toward the *nigrodha* tree. Just as she reached it, the sun rose across the plain and shone upon the sacred tree, making it glitter in the morning light. Punna started in surprise. At the foot of the tree sat a figure so emaciated that it looked as if a human face had been set upon a skeleton. And yet the face seemed to radiate holiness and nobility.

Thinking she had seen the god of the *nigrodha* tree, Punna turned on her heel and rushed back to tell her mistress. As Sujata listened to the maid's tale, a feeling of inexpressible joy rose within her. She thought, "The deity must have manifested himself in human form in order to accept our offerings personally."

Sujata and Punna filled a golden bowl to the brim with the fresh milk gruel and rushed to the *nigrodha* tree. Night had turned to day, and the holy man sat immersed in meditation amid the bright morning sunlight. The two women prostrated themselves before the shining figure and prepared reverently to offer the milk gruel.

Now, the figure the women thought to be the tree god was in fact Prince Siddhattha, who had been crown prince of the Shakyas but had left the palace in Kapilavatthu some six years earlier to seek enlightenment. Having traveled widely and sought enlightenment under many teachers, Siddhattha had selected the Grove of the Ascetics, near Senani, as the site of his final ascetic effort, resolving that he would not leave until he had attained perfect enlightenment.

He embarked on a severe fast, eating only one sesame seed and one grain of rice a day. When he entered the "breathless trance," in which normal breathing is suspended and the mind is concentrated upon itself, he would lose consciousness and fall to the ground. Awakening from his trance, he would continue his fast. This was an extreme form of asceticism, transcending the limits of normal human endurance. At times he felt he was but a step from the final goal of enlightenment; but when he emerged again from his trance, everything he thought he had achieved would vanish.

Calmly Siddhattha asked himself, "Will this extreme practice really lead to enlightenment? Even if I were able to extinguish all physical attachment and attain enlightenment in this way, my health would be destroyed and my life would be at an end. And so I would not be able to transmit my enlightenment to anyone else. What sense would there be in that—attaining enlightenment for myself alone, and then dying without helping others?"

Thus Siddhattha decided to abandon his extreme asceticism. Using his last reserves of energy, he stood up and dragged his body, caked with dirt and moss, to the nearby river. He bathed in its pure waters and then pulled himself up onto the bank by means of a tree root that extended over the stream. Sitting down beneath the great *nigrodha* tree, Siddhattha entered a state of deep meditation. His emaciated body, its hands and feet like slender tree branches, shone in the golden light of the rising sun.

It was at that moment that Punna had seen him and rushed back home to tell Sujata of her "vision." The holy man's appearance was indeed awe-inspiring. Sujata moved forward and timidly proffered the golden bowl of milk gruel. The man before them suddenly stretched forth his left hand and took the bowl; then slowly, as if savoring each mouthful, he drank the gruel.

Having drunk the gruel Sujata and Punna had prepared, Siddhattha felt new energy begin to spread throughout his body. Rising, he walked as far as the outskirts of Gaya, a short distance along the riverbank from the *nigrodha* tree. He seated himself beneath a tree that stood there and entered a profound state of meditation. At dawn of the seventh day after that, Siddhattha attained perfect enlightenment and thus became a buddha.

Soon people began to speak of the holy man Shakyamuni, who had attained a hitherto unknown degree of enlightenment and become a buddha. He was said to have converted the three Kassapa brothers, eminent ascetics in Uruvela, and then to have converted Sariputta and Moggallana, former disciples of Sanjaya, the most prominent thinker of the age, together with the rest of his two hundred and fifty disciples. The king of Magadha and most of the leading aristocrats had also become Shakyamuni's followers.

One day the Buddha visited Senani on a preaching tour. Hearing that the great sage had arrived, Sujata and her maid went to hear him speak. Sujata made her way to the front of the crowd and bowed reverently before the Buddha. But when she raised her head, she cried out in astonishment. Was this not the deity of the *nigrodha* tree, to whom she had offered milk gruel? She thought, "So it was not the tree god, after all, but the prince of the Shakyas who accepted my milk gruel that morning. He drank the gruel and later attained enlightenment, becoming a buddha. How fortunate we were to be able to make an offering to such a person!"

Sujata and Punna were barely able to contain their

joy and excitement as they listened to the sermon. When the Buddha had finished speaking, Sujata went forward and, bowing at his feet, made this request: "World-honored One, please accept me as a lay disciple. From this day forward I wish to take refuge in you and your holy teachings and to gain merit by making offerings to the monks for the rest of my life." Punna followed her mistress's example. The Buddha accepted them both.

In this way Sujata became the Buddha's first female lay disciple. From that day on she engraved the Buddha's words in her heart and never failed to observe them. She was devoted to her family, looked after the needs of her servants, and willingly did all she could for the entire household. In addition, she devoted herself to the practice of the Buddha's teaching and never neglected to make offerings to the monks. As a result, she was loved and respected not only by her own family but by all who met her, and passed the rest of her days in happiness and peace.

CHITTA
The Wavering Monk

Chitta-Hatthisariputta was a young farmer who lived in Savatthi, the capital of Kosala. Early each morning he set out for the fields just outside the city and worked until nightfall. One day, having finished all his work in the fields before noon, he decided to visit the nearby Jetavana Monastery, where Shakyamuni was staying. Shakyamuni was highly regarded by the people of the area, and the number of those who went to hear him preach grew daily. Chitta had been thinking that he would like to hear the man who, people said, had been born a prince of the Shakyas and had now become a buddha.

The monastery lay peacefully in a grove bathed in the clear light of autumn. It was utterly quiet; no one appeared to be about. Chitta stood before the monastery gate, taken aback by the silence. Then from behind him came a voice: "Is anything wrong?" Turning around in surprise, he saw an elderly monk with a warm smile on his face. He looked as if he had just come back from his daily begging rounds, since his bowl was filled with delicious-looking food.

Chitta gulped, and his stomach began to rumble. He

had done a full day's work already, and it was noon. Watching Chitta, the old monk smiled and said, "It must be thanks to some karmic bond from the past that we have been able to meet here like this. Why don't you share my lunch?" Chitta hesitated for a moment, but before he knew it he had stretched out his hand. The monk placed in it a morsel of food of the sort that a farmer like Chitta rarely had a chance to taste. It was indescribably delicious.

After that Chitta often recalled the splendid food the old monk had given him. When he was tired and hungry from working all day in the fields, he would say to himself, "Farmers like me have to work day after day till we're covered with dirt and sweat, yet we never get to eat such delicious food. But if you're a monk you can eat that way every day, and all you have to do is preach and go out begging."

His heavy labor in the fields came to seem more and more pointless. Finally Chitta decided to become a monk in order to escape hard work and lead a comfortable life. One day soon after, he visited the Jetavana Monastery and expressed his desire to join the Sangha. His request was transmitted to Shakyamuni, who quickly gave his consent, much to everyone's surprise.

And so Chitta's new life as a monk began. But he soon learned that the life of a Buddhist monk was not as easy as he had thought. First there were the various monastic precepts to be observed. One had to sit perfectly still in meditation from early morning to late night. Sometimes one had to go on begging rounds, visiting each house in Savatthi. Then there were tasks to perform for the senior monk who had been appointed one's teacher. And in one's free moments, one had to learn to recite the Dharma from memory. As for the fine meals Chitta had been looking forward to, he found that all he got day after day was gruel. Not once did he receive the kind of delicious food he had shared with the elderly monk on his first visit to the monastery.

After little more than a month, Chitta was ready to give up. He slipped quietly from the monastery one night and ran home; the next morning he returned to his work in the fields. But after two or three days a feeling of uneasiness began to assail him, like a cold wind blowing into a badly built house in winter. He began to long for the monastic life that had seemed so severe. The senior monks who took such pains to teach the novices their new way of life, and the life itself, so free from turmoil—now he realized how good it all was. Soon Chitta found himself on the road back to Jetavana.

He approached the monks' dormitory with great apprehension, but his fellow monks welcomed him as if nothing had happened. He was greatly relieved and vowed to himself that this time he would persevere with his training, no matter how rigorous it was, and would devote himself to the study of the Dharma. Chitta recalled that as a child he had been praised for his cleverness. He encouraged himself with the thought that if he worked hard, he too could become a good monk and attain enlightenment. He threw himself into religious practice with all his energy; but six months passed, and then a year, and still he found himself unable to free himself from troubling emotions. Laziness would overcome him periodically, and he would be drawn back toward the pleasures of the material world.

Overcome with shame, once again Chitta sneaked

away from the monastery under cover of darkness and ran home. He found, however, that he could not escape the feeling of emptiness in his heart, a feeling that grew stronger by the day. No matter what he did, he was assailed by an unbearable sense of loneliness. And so he was compelled to return again to the monastery. Having twice broken his vows and returned to lay life without permission, Chitta went before his fellow monks expecting to be treated as an apostate. But the eyes with which the monks gazed at him were kind, which encouraged him to begin yet again. He regretted his former lack of will and sincerely renewed his monastic vows.

How many times did he go through this process— wandering from the Way, then returning to the monastic life, then failing again? No matter how hard he tried, he seemed unable to conquer delusion. But in the process of falling away and returning, backsliding and then grasping hold of the truth again, Chitta gradually learned a great deal about the Dharma and eventually became the equal of the senior monks in knowledge and theoretical understanding. He began to expound the Dharma at the request of his fellow monks. And thus, unfortunately, he began to become proud.

On one occasion he was devoting himself to religious practice in Deer Park, near Varanasi in the land of Kasi, in company with Shakyamuni. The senior monks had all assembled there, as well, and were holding daily discussions on the Dharma in the lecture hall of the monastery. Chitta went to the lecture hall to hear the discussions, but, full of confidence in his own understanding of the Buddha's teachings, he broke into the discussions of the senior monks several times to put forward his own opinions. Annoyed at seeing the discussions interrupted, the senior monk Maha-Kotthita rebuked him: "Friend Chitta-Hatthisariputta, you must not break into the discussions of the senior monks to interject your own views. If you wish to express your opinions, you must wait till the others have finished speaking."

A monk who was friendly toward Chitta replied, "Venerable Maha-Kotthita, please do not humiliate Chitta. He is learned enough to join as an equal in your discussions—that is why he has tried to present his views here."

Maha-Kotthita nodded gravely and responded, "My friend, I know that Chitta has studied the Dharma carefully and is very learned. But there are many people who, while putting on a show of modesty in front of their teachers and other eminent people, are inwardly arrogant, deluding themselves into thinking that they have attained the level of nonretrogression, in which there is no danger of falling back into evil ways. They associate with worldly people, with kings and great lords, and with unbelievers; and gradually they are drawn into a worldly life and end by becoming full of greed and attachment. Thus it is very dangerous for one who has not yet attained the highest enlightenment to have too much contact with worldly people, even for the sake of expounding the Dharma."

Maha-Kotthita's words sprang from concern for Chitta's welfare, but Chitta paid little attention and, as a result, was to slip from the path again, and in a most serious way.

Chitta had gone with Shakyamuni to the land of Kuru, northwest of Kosala. He stayed in the village of Kammasadamma, preaching the Dharma to all the people of the area. Chitta was venerated by everyone and had many opportunities for friendly socializing. Gradually he came to feel a deep envy for the pleasant life of the lay people among whom he lived. He thought to himself that, having followed the religious life for years and being learned in the Dharma, surely he would not retrogress even if he did mingle with worldly people. But as he spent more and more time with lay people and unbelievers, he became hardened even to such grave breaches of the monastic precepts as drinking intoxicants and having physical contact with members of the opposite sex.

Reports of Chitta's misconduct reached the Sangha, and Ananda, the Buddha's personal attendant, visited Kammasadamma on his begging rounds to see for himself. Ananda arrived at dawn at the gate of the house where Chitta was said to be staying. Looking inside, he saw Chitta asleep, his monk's robe thrown aside, leaning against two beautiful young women, one on either side of him. He had been carousing all night and did not even realize that it was morning. Chitta became aware that someone was standing in the gateway. He stood up shakily, supported by the two women, and approached the gate. Then he recognized who it was who stood there.

His drunkenness seemed to slip away from him as he rubbed his eyes. No, there was no mistake—it was indeed Ananda standing there in the morning sunlight. Ananda gazed at him with eyes filled with sorrow. Chitta felt a shock run through his body. He threw himself down before Ananda and lay there, convulsed with sobs.

Returning from Chitta's house, Ananda reported what he had seen to Shakyamuni. He nodded and responded, "A man's mind is hard to control. Until he has truly attained the state of nonretrogression, he is in danger of being drawn back into the worldly life of pleasure if he relaxes his vigilance. If he lives among the worldly, he is liable to be drowned in a sea of lust, greed, and attachment. Nevertheless, Ananda, there is no need to worry. Chitta is now adrift on the sea of delusion owing to the heavy weight of his past karma. But seven days from now he will come to me and ask to be readmitted to the Sangha. And this time, he will attain enlightenment."

And so it was. Seven days later, Chitta came to Shakyamuni to ask to be readmitted as a low-ranking monk, expressing deep repentance for his wrongdoing. Chitta had slipped back into a worldly life again and again. Eventually, though, he came to realize that there was no path for him but the Dharma. Then, devoting himself singlemindedly to his practice, he was able to attain first the state of nonretrogression and then the enlightenment of an *arahant.*

Because of Chitta's past record, some monks could not believe that he had attained the state of nonretrogression. But he was not upset by such doubts. He simply continued to devote himself quietly to religious practice and went on preaching the Dharma. All his actions accorded with the Dharma. In time, no one doubted that he would no longer retrogress, and all his fellow monks came to respect him deeply. The *Dhammapada* records the following words of Shakyamuni in praise of Chitta, who gained enlightenment after learning to control his wayward mind: "It is good to tame the mind, which is difficult to control and flighty, rushing wherever it will; a tamed mind brings happiness."

SONA
The Loving Mother

In Savatthi, the capital of Kosala, there lived a woman named Sona, whom the people of the city always referred to as "she of the many children." She had been born into a rich merchant family and had been brought up comfortably by her loving parents. When she came of age, she married into one of the leading families of Savatthi and bore ten children. Now, it was not unusual for an Indian woman of that time to bear five or six children, some of whom would almost surely die because of poverty or illness. But to have ten children and rear them all safely, as Sona did, was most unusual. Moreover, all her children, boys and girls alike, were remarkably loving.

Sona's heart was filled with happiness as she watched her children grow. All her children were precious to her, and she enjoyed spending her time busily seeing to their needs. "My children are all the treasure I need," she would murmur to herself. Thus she reared her ten children to adulthood. First the oldest son married and set up his own household, and then the second son did the same. A little later the oldest daughter married into another family of the city. One after another, all the children married and left home. Finally only Sona, her aging husband, and a few servants remained in the spacious house.

One day Sona's husband announced abruptly that he was going to become a Buddhist monk. "Our sons and daughters have grown up and become independent," he said. "I've fulfilled my responsibilities as head of the household, and now I want to spend the rest of my life seeking the Way. I give you all my wealth; I leave everything in your hands." His decision, made after much careful thought, was unshakable. A short time later he entered the Sangha to follow more completely the Buddha's teaching.

After her husband's departure Sona felt a deep emptiness within. Her precious children, her treasures whom she had nurtured with such love and care, had gone away; now her husband had left, as well. Had his affection for her been weakened during the long years when she had devoted herself wholly to her children? She was now over fifty years old; what was left for her to do? A sense of the vanity of life swept over her.

Sona began to visit her children's homes more frequently. At first all her children and their spouses welcomed her, partly because they knew their father had left all his property to her. One day, when Sona was visiting her oldest son's house, her daughter-in-law said, "We're very happy to have you visit us so often, Mother. But we think it would be better if you'd come to live with us. And in that case, don't you agree it would be best to give us some of your property so we can handle it for you?"

Sona was happy at the thought of being able to live with her oldest son's family and readily agreed to hand over a portion of her holdings. When the other children learned of this, they all came forward urging her to come and live with their families, where she would be "taken care of best." Before long, Sona had divided all the property she had received from her husband among her children and their families. She was glad to do so if it meant staying close to her treasures.

However, once all the property had been divided up, the children's attitude showed a remarkable change, shifting from warm welcome to ill-concealed irritation. One day Sona fell ill and took to her bed at her oldest son's house. Five, then ten days passed with little improvement in her condition, and finally her daughter-in-law commented sarcastically, "You know, Mother, you have other children besides us. They've all been saying how much they want you to come and live with them. I think it's time to let them look after you for a while." Then she delivered poor Sona, gasping from pain and fatigue, to her second son's house. The second son and his wife looked after their ailing mother for four or five days and then took her to the third son's house. After three days there, she was moved on to her fourth son's; and so on. Sona was passed from house to house like an unwanted piece of baggage.

Sona was finally forced to face the fact that she had been rejected by all those she loved. She thought, "I've been cast aside even by the children I reared for so many years, caring more for them than I did for myself. Now, in my old age, I have no one to turn to. Is there anything reliable in this world of ours? How can I find the strength to go on living?"

Sitting alone in the vast, empty rooms of the house her husband had left her, now stripped of all its ornaments and furnishings, Sona moaned to herself. Then, rising with difficulty, she aimlessly left the house. Her feet carried her along the road her husband had taken when he left her, toward the Jetavana Monastery on the outskirts of the city.

Coming upon a nun in the monastery, Sona knelt before her. "Reverend sister," she said, "teach me how I should live from this day on. What should I rely upon?" Questioned by the nun, she revealed that she had reared ten children and was now left utterly alone. Then the nun explained to Sona the basic causes of her present suffering.

"How can I eliminate these causes within myself? Can I become free of them if I become a nun and engage in religious practice?" The image of the nun gravely nodding in answer to this question was etched on Sona's heart. Soon after, she presented herself to the Buddha and asked for admission to the Sangha. When she was tonsured as a sign of acceptance as a novice, she told herself, "Being so old, I must work twice as hard as the younger nuns if I am to gain enlightenment." She knew that if she wasted her time, she would end her life fruitlessly, without having attained her goal. She wanted to reach a state of peace, free of the bonds of passion, as quickly as possible.

To become a full-fledged nun, one had to pass through a two-year novitiate. Sona was kept busy with various tasks under the direction of nuns young enough to be her daughters. Rushing about from morning till night performing an endless succession of tasks, Sona obeyed willingly and did her best to fulfill her responsibilities. In the little free time remaining to her, she studied the Dharma. In the dead of night, after the other nuns had gone to sleep, she would grope her way from pillar to pillar till she reached the meditation hall, where she would sit practicing until dawn. If she relaxed her vigilance in the slightest, feelings of love and hate toward her husband and children would flood her mind. At such times she would throw herself with renewed energy into the deadly struggle with herself.

It was pitiful to watch her struggling so, an elderly woman whose hair was beginning to turn white. One day she heard a voice beside her say, "Sona, a hundred years of life in delusion is not worth one day of earnest striving that leads to enlightenment." Startled, Sona looked up and saw the Buddha.

She thought, "If I don't free myself from worldly bonds, I'll never find the truth. It's essential to cast aside self and concentrate on practice instant by instant—that's the only way!" At this thought, Sona felt a faint ray of light illuminate her heart. In her practice over the ensuing days, that light grew stronger and stronger; and one day Sona saw the world and herself within it—past, present, and future—flooded with a spiritual radiance. At last she had attained enlightenment.

She sat still, lost in meditation. When morning came, a young nun came and spoke to her: "We're leaving now. Please heat the water as usual. We'll need it when we come back." But when the nuns returned, Sona was still sitting in the same spot. In the kitchen the water was boiling, yet there was no sign of a fire on the hearth. There was a precept that within the Sangha one who had not yet attained enlightenment should not give orders to one who had already reached that state. So as not to involve the young nun in even an unintentional violation of that precept, Sona had caused the water to boil miraculously, through the use of the supernatural powers that often accompany enlightenment.

When the nuns understood this, they were amazed and rushed to tell the Buddha. He nodded calmly and praised Sona, saying, "Surely, Sona is foremost in practice among the nuns."

The following passage in the *Therigatha* is ascribed to Sona: "Having borne ten children in this material body, and then having become weak and aged, I approached a nun. She taught me of the elements of existence, the sense-bases, and the elements. Having heard these teachings, I cut off my hair and was ordained. When I was a novice my divine eye was purified. I knew my past, in what state I had lived before. Intent and well concentrated, I realized the truth of the Void. Immediately thereafter I attained complete liberation; I became tranquil, without clinging. The elements of existence, their nature known, continue to exist with roots cut off. Having an enduring foundation, I am immovable. There is now no renewed existence of delusion."

UGGA
The Cheerful Giver

Vesali, the capital of the Vajji confederation, was a prosperous commercial city where major trade routes converged. Many merchants who had amassed great fortunes through foreign trade lived there. Such men were given the respectful title of householder. Among their number was a man named Ugga. He possessed a great sailing ship, which he sent down the Ganges and into the vast ocean. He organized caravans to travel overland to distant lands to buy and sell. Such trade had made him immensely wealthy.

"Money's what counts in this world. With money you can make a grand lord, or even a king, get down on his knees before you. Everything is possible with money." This was Ugga's philosophy of life. He built himself a grand mansion in Vesali and installed in it his four attractive young wives. The wives looked after Ugga like faithful servants, seeing to his every need, fulfilling his every whim. In addition, he had numerous attendants who diligently obeyed their master's commands. Yet though Ugga seemed to have everything a man could desire, he felt that something was lacking. He wore clothes of the finest Kasi silk, and his tables were loaded with the richest foods and the rarest wines, but he remained unsatisfied. Even after searching out the loveliest female entertainers in Vesali as attendants, singers, and dancers, he felt that something was lacking in his life. Indeed, the more he tried to enjoy himself to the full, the more he was assailed by a sense of emptiness and futility.

One day Ugga had the town's most beautiful dancing girls sent to a park on the outskirts of the city where a boisterous party was in progress. But still he was not satisfied. "Wine is best," he cried; "it brings joy to the heart. Give me some more—bring on the finest wines!" People were shocked at such goings-on in broad daylight, but Ugga did not care. He drank until he was dizzy, then laid his head in the lap of one of his attendants and fell into a drunken sleep. When he awoke, the sun was beginning to set in the western sky. Looking around, he saw the singers and dancers lying in slovenly fashion on the ground asleep, some of them mumbling incoherently in their dreams. Suddenly Ugga was overcome by an intense loathing. Pushing the women aside, he stumbled on uncertain legs into the depths of the wooded park.

He was still quite drunk, and the steadily darkening trees seemed to shift like figures in a dream. All at once a figure appeared before him, a figure that seemed to emit a strange radiance. Ugga thought he might be dreaming, but the apparition turned out to be a solitary ascetic sitting immersed in meditation. Moving closer, Ugga looked directly at the ascetic's face. As he looked, he felt as if a cool breeze were blowing through him. It was as if all the accumulated spiritual pollution within him had been washed away. The atmosphere of the place itself seemed somehow purified.

The ascetic was Shakyamuni, who was then staying at the Gabled Hall in the depths of the forest. Though already advanced in years, he continued his frequent preaching trips, winning many converts in Magadha, Kosala, and the Vajji confederation. All this Ugga knew. But despite his dissatisfaction with his present way of life, Ugga had never had any particular interest in Shakyamuni or his teachings. "This thing they call enlightenment," he would say to himself, "what good is it for getting what I want out of life—money and pleasure!"

Faced with the Buddha himself, however, Ugga could not help being impressed by the nobility of his appearance. Shakyamuni spoke to the awe-struck man: "Ugga, you are the envy of everyone because of your wealth and position. Yet you seem to be filled with discontent, unable to find what you are really looking for. But there is a way to satisfy the kinds of longings that neither wealth nor rank can gratify. If, as a merchant, you desire an object, do you not pay its price in gold and thus obtain it? If you want something of value, you must give something to gain it. To gain true happiness, you must keep the precepts. Generous giving is also a good way to gain what you really desire. Through its practice you will find true happiness in this life and gain rebirth in the heavenly realms in the next."

Ugga became excited at these words and asked, "Is it truly possible for a human being to be reborn in the heavenly realms? If so, I'd do anything to gain that. Please tell me what I must do."

Then Shakyamuni explained to Ugga the five precepts that the Buddhist lay believer must observe: to refrain from taking life, stealing, indulging in sexual

misconduct, lying, and drinking intoxicants. Ugga was
the type of person who had to act upon an idea immediately. Just meeting the Buddha in the woods had
spiritually refreshed him. The vague, unpleasant feelings that had burdened him for so long had quite
vanished. Merely hearing the Buddha's teaching once
had left him with an inner feeling of deep satisfaction.

Having decided to follow the Buddha's teaching,
Ugga promptly assembled his wives in his private
apartments and said, "It will seem rather sudden to
you, no doubt, but I have decided to become a lay disciple of the Buddha and to observe the five precepts
from this day forward. Therefore I can no longer live
with you as man and wife. If you wish to leave my
household, you may do so. If you wish to marry into
another household in Vesali, I will help you do so. If
you wish to return to your own family, I will send you
back safely, with enough money to live on for the rest
of your life. And anyone who wishes to join me as a
disciple of the Buddha, observing the five precepts, is
welcome to remain here with me."

From that day on, Ugga made strict observance of
the five precepts the center of his life. At first he found
that sensual desire was his constant companion. But as
he continued to visit the Buddha and listen to his
teachings on the Four Noble Truths and the Eightfold
Path, his desire began gradually to fade. In time he
came to find his greatest pleasure in doing good—in using the wealth gained from trading to provide food for
the poor and offerings for the monks. The more he
gave, the more joy he experienced; he felt himself
growing spiritually richer day by day.

Ugga's charity became famous not only among the
inhabitants of Vesali but also among the merchants

and travelers who journeyed there from distant lands. Each day he had some twenty extra places set at his table for visiting monks, and five times a month he invited all the monks staying at the Gabled Hall to come and receive offerings. Nor was his charity limited to the monks. If any visitor to Vesali became ill, he provided medicine; if he came across someone who lacked the necessities of life, he provided him or her with food and clothing.

Several years after Ugga had begun the practice of charity, there came a day of great sorrow: Shakyamuni died. Ugga was overcome with grief until he began to recall the teachings he had heard directly from Shakyamuni. Then he reaffirmed his commitment to the teachings and resolved to devote the rest of his life to the practices of generous giving and self-purification.

But troubles seldom come singly in this world. Soon after that Ugga's great sailing ship met with a violent storm on its return from a foreign port and sank with an untold quantity of gold and other precious goods on board. Ugga did not seem particularly upset at the news, however, and continued to give generously to those in need. It was clear to everyone that his resources were shrinking daily and that unless he curbed his generosity he would soon be ruined.

News of this reached the ears of Ananda, who had served as the Buddha's personal attendant for years and now guided the Sangha after the Buddha's death. Ananda was visiting Vesali, and the monks living in the Gabled Hall requested that he urge Ugga to stop his practice of charity for the time being. Knowing that the monks had Ugga's interests at heart, Ananda conveyed their concern to him.

Ugga welcomed Ananda and, when he had heard his

counsel, bowed reverently and replied, "I am most grateful for your kindness, and I am truly sorry that I cannot do as you suggest. Please explain to the other monks why I cannot: I learned from the Buddha himself the importance of generous giving, and through this teaching was freed from the bonds of excessive desire. Having become a lay disciple, I vowed to keep the five precepts and to gain merit by helping to propagate Buddhism. In particular, I vowed to become a wheel-rolling king, an ideal ruler, in a future life. So you see, even if I lose all my material possessions, I cannot give up my hope of becoming a wheel-rolling king."

Ananda understood at once the depth and sincerity of Ugga's desire to follow the path to enlightenment taught by the Buddha at whatever cost to himself. Encouraged by Ananda, Ugga continued his strict practice of virtue and was praised by all the monks and the people of Vesali as a model lay disciple. In the end his fortunes recovered, and he became more prosperous than ever.

VISAKHA
The Woman of Great Generosity

A grand bridal procession was about to enter Savatthi, the capital of Kosala. At its head was Visakha, the daughter of Dhananjaya, who was a rich man of Saketa, a city south of Savatthi. The bystanders stared in amazement. In a fine carriage sat the bride, clothed in gorgeous robes and adorned with gems; next came carriages bearing numerous maidservants, followed by carts carrying a dowry of 590 million pieces of gold, as well as objects of gold, silver, and bronze, sumptuous clothing, oils, perfumes, bales of rice, and agricultural implements. In all, there were some five hundred carriages and carts. In front and to the rear of the column marched soldiers personally led by King Pasenadi.

As the long procession entered the city, the people gave a great shout and pressed forward. No wonder they were excited. Visakha had come to be the bride of Punnavaddhana, the son of Migara, a prominent citizen of Savatthi. Her own father was a man of almost inconceivable wealth who had moved from his native land of Anga to Kosala at the personal invitation of King Pasenadi. Visakha had been reared in great luxury, surrounded by servants; she also had a reputation for high intelligence, as well as a beauty that captivated everyone who saw her. When she was seven years old, Shakyamuni had visited Saketa on one of his preaching tours. At her father's suggestion Visakha had journeyed there from her home in distant Anga, accompanied by five hundred maidservants and five hundred carriages, to hear the Buddha's teaching, which she had understood clearly.

Migara of Savatthi had been frantically seeking an appropriate bride for his son. Despite his parents' urging, the young man showed not the slightest interest in marriage. When pressed, he would reply, "If you can find me a woman with hair as glossy as the feathers of the peacock and lips as luscious as sweet fruit, with teeth like pearls and skin as soft as the petals of the lotus flower—then, and only then, will I marry." How in the world could they find such a woman? Nevertheless, they sent emissaries to search everywhere, and finally they found her: Visakha, the daughter of Dhananjaya.

Migara went at once to see Dhananjaya and gained his consent to the marriage of Visakha and Punnavaddhana. All preparations for receiving the new bride were speedily completed, and Visakha, resplendent in her bridal robes, set out for Savatthi, accompanied by Migara and guarded by King Pasenadi and the royal troops. A grand wedding ceremony took place at the Migara family mansion. Gifts came from the king, the ministers, and the townspeople. But Visakha took the gifts and divided them among the needy. Everyone praised both her beauty and her character.

Everything went smoothly in Visakha's new life until one day her father-in-law came to her apartments, requesting her, as his new daughter-in-law, to greet some visiting holy men. Thinking they must be the Buddha's disciples, Visakha made sure her hair and clothing were in good order and then hurried to the guest hall. But the holy men who awaited her there were in fact naked ascetics. Migara was a devotee of these ascetics and frequently made offerings to them. When Visakha saw them, she turned on her heel and returned to her own apartments, saying, "The true holy men in this age are the Buddha and his disciples. The ascetics in the guest hall are not holy men—if they were, they would not appear before others in so shameless a manner."

When they heard these remarks, the naked ascetics were enraged and complained to Migara. They asked him why he had accepted a follower of Shakyamuni as his daughter-in-law and urged him to drive her away at once. But to do so would be to incur the wrath not only of her rich father but also of King Pasenadi himself. All Migara could do was try to smooth things over by saying that Visakha was still young and immature and that she would change her ways before long.

One morning a few days after this incident, several Buddhist monks came to the door for alms just as Visakha was serving breakfast to her father-in-law. Migara pretended not to notice them and went on eating his gruel. Visakha moved to one side so that Migara could have a clear view of the monks, but her father-in-law continued eating his breakfast. Finally Visakha went to the gate and apologized: "I'm terribly sorry, but we have nothing we can offer you today. My father-in-law is breakfasting on leftovers."

At the word "leftovers," Migara lost his temper. "What do you mean, leftovers!" he shouted. "Visakha, you are no longer my daughter-in-law. Get out this instant!" But Visakha calmly replied, "When a married woman is sent back to her parents' home by her in-laws, some explanation must be given for why this was done. My parents have appointed eight guardians for me. I would like you to ask their opinion as to whether I have acted wrongly."

Migara agreed to consult the guardians. When they were gathered together, he appealed to them in loud, aggrieved tones: "Visakha humiliated me in front of some Buddhist monks by saying that I was eating left-overs for breakfast!"

"No, that is not true, Father. I saw that you were eating your own breakfast without making offerings to the Buddhist monks waiting at your gate, so I said to them that you apparently were not concerned about acquiring merit for the future but were content with the leftover merit of your past good deeds."

Hearing this explanation, Migara was at a loss for words, and the eight guardians agreed that there was no ill intent in what Visakha had said. Then Visakha addressed her father-in-law again: "I hope you see, Father, that I did not intend to offend you. But I was reared in a pious Buddhist family, and I can't bear to stay in a household where one may not make offerings to Buddhist monks. I ask your permission to go."

When Migara saw Visakha stand up to leave, he became agitated and said, "Wait a minute, please. I was at fault. You have been a perfect wife to my son. Please reconsider and stay on, for the good of the family. Of course you may make offerings to the monks whom you respect so highly." So Visakha remained in her husband's family, on the condition that she could make offerings to the Buddhist monks as she wished.

She immediately set out to visit the Buddha, who

was then staying at the Jetavana Monastery, and asked
to be allowed to make offerings of food in the name of
her father-in-law. The Buddha readily agreed. But
when the appointed day came and the Buddha and his
disciples arrived and began to receive the food, Migara
refused to welcome them. When, the meal over, the
Buddha was about to preach, Visakha sent a message
to Migara asking him to come and hear the sermon.
Migara went out of curiosity, but as he listened, each
word that the Buddha spoke seemed directed to him
personally. Migara was deeply moved by what he
heard, and when the sermon was over he found
himself going forward to bow at the Buddha's feet.

"How noble is the doctrine you teach!" he exclaimed. "Now I understand why Visakha reveres
you so highly. I too wish to take refuge in the
Three Treasures—the Buddha, the Dharma, and the
Sangha—and gain merit by making offerings to the
Sangha for the rest of my life." Then, going to his
daughter-in-law, he pressed her hand and said in a
voice filled with emotion, "Visakha, from today on
you are not my daughter-in-law but my mother—my
mother in the Dharma." And from then on, Visakha
was known as Migaramata, "Mother of Migara."

Having brought her new family to faith in Buddhism, Visakha became even more devoted to the
Three Treasures. In addition, she followed her father-
in-law's instructions to the letter, serving her family
with the utmost devotion. Over the years she bore
twenty children, ten boys and ten girls, all of whom
grew up strong and healthy. Visakha also made a vow
before the Buddha to practice the eight forms of
generous giving for the rest of her life: "I vow to provide outer garments for the monks' use during the

rainy season. I vow to provide food for monks who are visiting this monastery and for monks who are preparing to leave on their travels, for monks who are ill and for the monks who care for them. I vow to provide medicine and gruel for the ill. And finally, I vow to provide bathing garments for the nuns."

One day there was a festival, and Visakha dressed in her finest clothes and visited the Jetavana Monastery. Leaving her bejeweled outer robe in the care of her maid, she entered the hall where the Buddha was preaching. After the sermon, she visited the monks' quarters to see if there were any monks who were ill or about to set out on a journey. She and her maid entirely forgot about the robe. On the way home, she realized that the maid had left it at the monastery.

At that time Ananda was in charge of looking after the monastery, and as he made his rounds that day he saw the gorgeous robe lying forgotten in one of the rooms. He hung it on the railing of the staircase, and soon afterward Visakha's maid rushed in and asked in a breathless, nervous voice, "Reverend sir, have you by any chance seen my lady Visakha's robe somewhere around here? It is covered with jewels—you would recognize it at once."

"Why, yes. I just hung it on the railing of the staircase. You'd better go and get it right away."

"Then you yourself touched the robe?"

"Yes. I picked it up and hung it on the railing. Why? Is anything the matter?"

The maid answered, "In that case, I cannot take the robe back with me. My mistress said that even if I found the robe, if a senior monk had touched it, it should belong to the Sangha. She said that in that case I should respectfully offer it to the monastery."

So it happened that Visakha's robe was donated to the Sangha. It was offered for sale, but since it was worth 90 million gold pieces, there were no buyers. In the end Visakha herself redeemed it. Loading the gold pieces into a carriage, she went to the monastery and asked the Buddha how the money should be spent. He replied that it should be used to build another monastery. Visakha then bought a plot of land on the eastern outskirts of Savatthi and gave another 90 million gold pieces to build the monastery itself. When the buildings were completed, she contributed 90 million more to buy furnishings and utensils. In all, she gave 270 million gold pieces to the Sangha for the new monastery.

The construction of the monastery was directed by Moggallana, foremost in supernatural powers of the Buddha's disciples. With the help of his marvelous abilities, a splendid two-story monastery with five hundred cells on each level was completed within nine months. The new monastery, set in a quiet park, was named Migaramata Hall in honor of the donor. Together with the Jetavana Monastery, on the southern outskirts of the city, it became a center for the propagation of the Buddha's teachings in the Savatthi area.

One evening Visakha visited the newly finished monastery accompanied by many of her children and grandchildren. The Buddha praised her in the following words: "Just as many kinds of wreaths can be made from a heap of flowers, so many good things may be achieved by one born in human form." Visakha, by believing in and practicing the teachings she had received from Shakyamuni, was able to lead a full and happy life, praised by the Buddha as foremost among women in giving.

CHANNA
The Former Slave

A great many monks were gathered to hear the teachings of Shakyamuni, who was spending the rainy season at the Jetavana Monastery. A man named Channa was one of their number. Every day the Buddha preached the Dharma, and the monks strained to hear each word he spoke. Among the monks were two who were especially revered by the others: Sariputta, foremost in wisdom, and Moggallana, foremost in supernatural powers. Watching them, Channa's heart seethed with envy.

Having heard the Buddha's teachings, each of the monks devoted himself to a particular kind of religious exercise. Some did seated meditation, entering a deep trance. Others learned to recite the Buddha's sermons by heart. Some engaged in study and discussion of the theoretical aspects of the Dharma. Others sought the guidance of the senior monks concerning difficult points. Sariputta and Moggallana in particular were always surrounded by eager young inquirers.

This galled Channa. He had originally been a slave at the royal court of Kapilavatthu, the capital of the Shakyas. When the Buddha, who had formerly been

the crown prince of the Shakyas, first revisited Kapilavatthu after attaining enlightenment, Channa caught
a glimpse of him and was deeply impressed. He vowed
to become a disciple of this holy man.

How could he, a slave, be admitted to the Sangha?
Still, as he watched the sons of the great families of the
Shakyas become monks, he could not contain himself.
He summoned up all his courage and went before
Shakyamuni, saying, "I too wish to enter the Sangha,
but I am a low-caste Sudra. . . . Probably there is no
hope for me. . . ." His voice faltered. But the Buddha
said, "Come, Channa, and join us." Then he told
Channa how, according to the Dharma, there was no
distinction of class or caste; how any man could attain
enlightenment if only he revered the Three Treasures
of the Buddha, the Dharma, and the Sangha and, earnestly keeping the precepts, sought the Way. Channa
gazed at the Buddha's face as he spoke. And long
after, whenever he recalled that look of profound compassion, he felt a kind of peace within himself.

Just as the Buddha had said, in the Sangha there
were men who had been merchants or landowning
Brahmans, men of great wealth who had given up everything to enter the community. There were noblemen who had left their beautiful wives behind. All of
them wore the same coarse robes and went about with
begging bowls. And since Channa was one of the earliest to enter the Sangha, all those who had entered
after him paid him respect.

"At the court, I was ordered about and looked down
on by everyone. But from now on, everything will be
different." So Channa thought; and, since he was
treated courteously by people of all ranks within the

Sangha, he gradually began to feel more and more proud of his position. Now, Sariputta and Moggallana had entered the Sangha at around the same time as he, yet the younger monks always sought them out as mentors, not Channa. He began to feel insulted, and finally he started criticizing Sariputta and Moggallana publicly. When the Buddha heard of this, he summoned Channa and asked him why he was acting in this way. Being reproved by the Buddha himself, Channa received a salutary shock and was so ashamed that he could hardly raise his head.

For some time after this, he controlled his feelings and worked hard at religious practice. But after a while the old feelings of envy flared up as strongly as ever whenever he saw Sariputta and Moggallana. Several young, immature monks fed Channa's folly with their flattering comments. Thus Channa started to attack the two senior monks once more. The news reached the Buddha, and again Channa repented of his wrongdoing when faced with a direct rebuke from his teacher. But his repentance was always short lived. After he had committed the same fault three times, Shakyamuni reprimanded him sharply: "Channa, Sariputta and Moggallana are, in fact, your best friends in the Dharma. Do not be misled by foolish and mean-spirited people."

When the rainy season had ended and the hills and fields of Kosala lay bright under the hot sun, Shakyamuni left the Jetavana Monastery to go on a preaching journey. The monks too left for various destinations. Channa found himself following in the Buddha's footsteps. He went south from Savatthi, past Saketa, to Varanasi, a great commercial city on the banks of the Ganges in the land of Kasi. Then, traveling upriver, he arrived in Kosambi, a prosperous trade center and the capital of the kingdom of Vamsa.

Everywhere he went, Channa was well received, since the local people were glad to welcome a disciple of the Buddha, who had just passed that way and moved their hearts with his preaching. But Channa believed he himself had become an eminent monk, worthy of receiving the reverence of lay people on his own account. While Shakyamuni was resting from his long journey at the Ghosita Monastery, in Kosambi, Channa finally caught up with him and stayed for a few days. A certain rich man welcomed him very hospitably and made a request: "Reverend Channa, please stay here and preach the Dharma. I would like to build a monastery for you. Kindly choose the site and give directions as to how you want it built."

Channa was overjoyed. "At last I'm beginning to get the same respect from people as Sariputta and Moggallana," he thought. Walking about Kosambi, he discovered a large *nigrodha* tree that looked several hundred years old. Deciding it would make good lumber for the new monastery, he hired a workman to cut it down. Unfortunately, it was a sacred tree, revered by the people of the area for generations. Furious at Channa's ill-considered act, the townspeople went to the Ghosita Monastery and complained to Shakyamuni. He summoned Channa and chided him: "Do you think it is right for a monk, who is supposed to preach the Dharma to the people and lead them in the way of peace, to belittle something that is sacred to them? Acts like that injure the Dharma and endanger the Sangha."

Channa was downcast for a time, but soon the splendid three-story monastery was completed and he was overjoyed. He decided to add a fine roof, but no sooner had the roof been completed than the building collapsed under its weight and several workmen were injured. Despite all this, Channa's folly only grew. He had a layman donate a grand bed, such as princes and noblemen sleep on, for his own use. He refused to attend the biweekly Ceremony of Repentance, saying that he had no offenses to confess.

Channa simply could not overcome his weaknesses. He continued to sin, repent, then break his promise to the Buddha again and again, even into old age. Shortly before the Buddha's death, in Kusinara, he called his attendant, Ananda, to his side and instructed him that the monks of the Sangha must no longer converse with Channa under any circumstances. If he were to address them, they should not reply, but remain silent. Ananda asked why he had come to this decision, and the Buddha replied, "Channa is still deeply enmeshed in delusion. As long as I am in this world, I can correct him and keep him in check. But after I enter nirvana, that will no longer be possible. Somehow we must awaken Channa. To do that, we have to separate him from the Sangha for a time and make him take stock of himself."

The news of the Buddha's death quickly reached Channa, who was on a preaching tour in a nearby region. Hurrying to Kusinara, he asked Ananda for the details of the Buddha's death. But Ananda, who had always been so kind and friendly, did not answer, averting his eyes with a pained expression.

"Is he so grief-stricken he can't say a word?" wondered Channa. But when all the other monks refused to speak to him, Channa's surprise turned to anger.

He thought they had decided to shun him after the Buddha's death. Channa angrily left on a preaching tour, but the monks whom he encountered on his journey also avoided all contact as soon as they caught sight of him. Channa was nonplused at his fellow monks' silence. He had always been prone to loneliness, and such treatment was worse than any physical torture. He could not fathom the reason for this icy wall of silence.

One day Channa found himself in Deer Park, near Varanasi, where the Buddha had preached his first sermon. Suddenly he recalled that seated meditation was effective in overcoming perturbation. So Channa seated himself beneath a large tree in Deer Park and entered deep meditation. Several days passed as he struggled with his feeling of loneliness at being abandoned by everyone. One day, shortly before dawn, a flash of realization pierced him: "I've been the slave of my passions all this time. The Buddha gave us the Four Noble Truths as a means of becoming free from such selfish passions. I've been proudly preaching those truths to others without practicing them myself. I've spent all my energy vilifying others; I haven't ever really confronted myself."

A chain that had fettered Channa's heart snapped, and he realized how foolish he had been. He began also to see the reason for his fellow monks' apparent ostracism. Channa left Deer Park and went straight to the Ghosita Monastery, where Ananda was staying. Throwing himself at Ananda's feet, he begged forgiveness. He also asked Ananda to instruct him again concerning the way to achieve true peace of mind.

Ananda gazed at Channa and nodded gravely. Then he told him what the Buddha had said for his benefit just before dying. "The Buddha cared so much about me, his most foolish disciple, even at the hour of his death?" Channa murmured. For the first time he realized the depth of the Buddha's compassion.

Ananda instructed Channa in the Three Treasures and the Eightfold Path once again, slowly and carefully. The teachings refreshed Channa's spirit, like water moistening the parched earth, and he was able at last to attain the state of nonretrogression. From that time on he devoted himself to religious practice, finally attaining the state of an *arahant* and winning the veneration of all who knew him. Channa's joy at attaining enlightenment is recorded as follows in the *Theragatha:* "Having heard the excellent teachings of the great one, taught by the one who has supreme knowledge, I practiced the Way in order to attain the state of deathlessness. He indeed has followed to the end the path to absolute bliss."

DHAMMADINNA
The Conqueror of the Passions

Dhammadinna was on the balcony of her house, awaiting the return of her husband, Visakha, as she did every day. Visakha was an immensely rich citizen of Rajagaha, the capital of Magadha, and a close friend of King Bimbisara. He was deeply in love with his beautiful young wife. She had been born into an upper-class family in Rajagaha and reared in the most comfortable circumstances.

Now the streets of the city lay spread out before her, bathed in soft twilight. When she saw her husband wending his way through the streets toward home, she leaned out over the railing. Visakha, coming home from a hard day's work, would usually look up and give her a warm smile. But for some reason, on this particular day he did not even look in her direction. Dhammadinna ran to the head of the stairs and waited as her husband came slowly up. She stood there with her arms outstretched, hardly able to wait for his embrace, but Visakha did not so much as touch her. "What can be wrong?" she wondered. "Did something unpleasant happen at work? But even so, he's not the sort of man to take it out on me."

Dhammadinna hurried to prepare for dinner. But during the meal her husband remained silent, though he usually praised her cooking. Finally she asked him, "Today when you came home you didn't even speak to me. Is there something I've been doing wrong? If so, I beg you to tell me what it is."

At last Visakha spoke: "No, you haven't done anything wrong. It's only that I made up my mind today not to touch a woman and not to take pleasure in what I eat. I've vowed to follow the Pure Practices taught by the Buddha."

Visakha, together with his friend King Bimbisara, had long been a lay disciple of the Buddha. On this day, after finishing his business, he had listened to a sermon given by the Buddha in the Bamboo Grove Monastery, on the outskirts of Rajagaha, and had come to realize that to attain true peace of mind he would have to follow the Pure Practices even though he was a layman. Entering a state of deep meditation, he had resolved never to waver in his vow.

"I've resolved to observe the Pure Practices as carefully as a monk even though I'm a layman. So I can no longer live with you as man and wife. I leave all my property in your hands—do with it as you wish. You may stay here as before, or you may return to your parents' home, taking with you as much money as you need for the rest of your life."

Dhammadinna was stunned by her husband's words. She asked herself, "Is it possible that he's going to leave me—the husband who's loved me so tenderly, and whom I've served so faithfully all these years?" She felt as if she had been plunged into hell itself. At the same time, she realized how firm Visakha's resolve was, for he had long been a devoted disciple of the Buddha. Something began to stir within her, and she thought, "Why don't I too devote myself to the Buddha's teachings, since my husband has found such joy in following them?" The teachings of the Buddha, which she had often heard from her husband, seemed to well up within her and strengthen her resolve.

Riding in the golden palanquin that her husband had bought for her, Dhammadinna entered a convent near the Bamboo Grove Monastery. She told herself, "Now that I've become a nun, I must endure rigorous discipline and strive to attain enlightenment as quickly as possible. I must not lag behind my former husband, who, though a layman, has taken upon himself the strictest observance of the precepts."

A nun's life was far more difficult than she had ever imagined, having been born and reared in a wealthy family. Nonetheless, she persevered. During her arduous practice in the convent outside Rajagaha, she would often think back to her old life and the husband from whom she had parted. She would be deep in meditation when suddenly her husband's face would float before her, and she would find herself wondering where he was at that moment and what he was doing. To conquer these thoughts, which seemed to draw her back to her former life, Dhammadinna decided to leave Rajagaha. She moved to an isolated village, where she spent her time meditating and going on begging rounds.

One day a passing merchant, seeing her, asked the villagers, "Are you content to see that beautiful young nun practicing austerities in this winter cold in just a thin summer robe? Why don't we take up a collection and buy her a nice warm robe?" The villagers agreed and asked Dhammadinna what kind of robe she would like.

Dhammadinna suggested they buy one costing about five hundred gold pieces. To Dhammadinna, who had been the wife of a very wealthy man, this seemed a modest sum, but it soon became the talk of the convent. Nuns were committed to poverty, and the others criticized Dhammadinna for going on begging rounds dressed "like the wife of a state minister." Eventually this talk reached the ears of the Buddha himself. He summoned Dhammadinna, inquired into the facts of the case, and then admonished her sternly: "When a nun accepts a robe from a lay person, it should be one worth no more than four gold pieces."

Dhammadinna felt deeply ashamed. She realized anew how strongly attached she was to material things. "Weak woman that I am," she thought, "I've always relied on my husband's high social status and his love for me, and taken jewelry and fine clothing for granted. That shows how enslaved I've been to worldly pleasures, bound fast by the chains of my selfish desires. And those attachments have blocked my path to enlightenment." At that very moment she felt that something within her had been set free. She realized that Visakha had been able to advance spiritually while remaining a layman precisely because he had had the will to follow the Buddha's teachings, even at the cost of his great wealth and position. From that day on, she too would abandon all attachments, seeing and hearing nothing but the Buddha's teachings. She would give up all interest in self and would practice strictly in accordance with the Buddha's words.

From then on, Dhammadinna cared nothing for what she wore or how she appeared to others. She observed each and every rule and precept taught by the Buddha. Little by little, she could feel the various obstacles that surrounded her slip away and disappear. Then one day she felt herself emerge into a new and wider world. Nothing bound or limited her. Dhammadinna had attained the state of an *arahant*.

There was no longer any need for her to live alone in an isolated village. She returned to the convent outside Rajagaha to pay reverence to the Buddha and to tell as many people as possible about the wondrous state of enlightenment she had attained.

Hearing that she had returned, Visakha went to visit her. Paying reverence to his former wife, he asked, "Sister Dhammadinna, I have some questions I would like to ask. May I?"

"Friend Visakha, ask anything you like."

"We always speak of our selves, but what in fact is the self according to the Buddha?"

"Visakha, the self is made up of five elements or aggregates: form, sensation, conceptions, volitions, and consciousness. This is the teaching of the Buddha."

"What is the basis of these five aggregates?"

"It is craving: the desire for physical pleasure and attachment to anything."

Now, Visakha had gone to see Dhammadinna out of concern that she, used to a life of luxury, might be suffering extreme hardship in her new life as a nun. How surprised he was at the ease and confidence with which she responded to his questions. He saw at once that she had attained a level of understanding far beyond his own. He went on to ask her about the Four Noble Truths and the Eightfold Path, and her replies were as clear and pointed as a sharp knife that cuts through the stalk of a lotus plant.

Dhammadinna had severed all attachments. The Buddha praised her, saying, "She who possesses nothing and is possessed by nothing in the past, present, or future—such a one I call a true nun." She made it her practice to travel widely on preaching missions and thus came to be known as foremost among nuns skilled in preaching.

One rainy season Dhammadinna was staying at the convent outside Savatthi, the capital of Kosala. Soldiers under the command of King Pasenadi of Kosala were lodged nearby with their families. The land was at peace, and the soldiers had time on their hands, which they spent gambling. They gambled away so much of their pay that their wives often had no decent clothes to wear. Dhammadinna told the soldiers and their wives that they should save half their pay each month before allowing themselves to spend a penny. When they began to follow her advice, they found their daily lives were much more comfortable. Soon the soldiers' families were quite well off. Pleased and grateful, they asked permission to make offerings of food to Dhammadinna. But she urged them to make offerings instead to the Buddha, who was then at the Jetavana Monastery, and she taught them the importance of taking refuge in the Three Treasures.

Through Dhammadinna the soldiers came to believe in the Buddha's teachings; and when they learned that taking life was the greatest of sins, they even began to carry sieves with them, just like monks, to avoid inadvertently swallowing any small insects that might be in their drinking water.

One day news came of a rebellion on the border of

Kosala. King Pasenadi was about to dispatch troops to put it down, when one of his ministers told him it would be no use sending those troops to the border region. He explained that they were devout Buddhists, loath to kill even an insect in their drinking water.

The king called his troops together and questioned them: "It seems you hesitate to kill even insects. Can you then fight against the rebels?"

"Yes, Your Majesty. It is our duty to fight those who break the king's just laws."

The soldiers were sent to the border and soon found themselves facing the rebel army. They immediately entered the Meditation on Compassion, which aims at arousing benevolent, merciful thoughts in both oneself and others. One who has fully entered this state cannot be burned by fire or pierced by a blade or killed by poison. Finally, the spirit of belligerence began to leave the rebel troops, and the insurrection ended without a sword being drawn or an arrow loosed.

"May one be earnest, truly determined, and mindful. One whose thought is not hindered by sensual pleasures is called 'one who rows against the current.'" These words in the *Therigatha* are attributed to Dhammadinna. Truly, in her long pursuit of the Way, she rowed against the current of the passions, seeking to purify both herself and all those she encountered.

KUTADANTA
The Brahman Who Learned the True Meaning of Sacrifice

It was Vesakha, the fifth month of the lunar calendar, and the village of Khanumata in the kingdom of Magadha was busy with preparations for the Grand Sacrifice. It was to take place in three days, with King Bimbisara as the sponsor. A great altar to the gods had been set up in the village square. Workers, covered with sweat and urged on by the cruel lash of the overseer, rushed to put the finishing touches to the altar. Men strained like oxen to pull the heavy carts loaded with auspicious grasses and grains to be offered during the ceremony. A great many animals—oxen, goats, sheep, and fowl—were being brought into the square as sacrificial offerings. The animals trembled and uttered sad cries, as if they knew the fate awaiting them.

Kutadanta heard all this from the balcony of his mansion. He was a Brahman who had received the village of Khanumata as a private holding from King Bimbisara. In addition, he had many young disciples who had been drawn to him by his immense learning. It was he who was to preside over the Grand Sacrifice.

As he gazed down on the square being readied for the ceremony, though, his face clouded. "Only three more days until the Grand Sacrifice," he thought. "There must be no slips. Yet when I think how many people are slaving away at these preparations, and how many animals will be killed, I feel uneasy."

Kutadanta was well versed in the conduct of the traditional Brahman ceremonies, but it was the first time he would preside over the Grand Sacrifice with King Bimbisara in attendance. His uneasiness continued to mount. Soon it was the day before the sacrifice. Kutadanta looked down at the plaza from his balcony and saw something that amazed him. A great crowd was running along a side street toward the outskirts of the village, away from the plaza with its festive decorations. Old men, young women, farmers with their hoes—all were rushing away from the village square.

One of his disciples reported that the villagers were going to Ambalatthika Park, at the edge of the village, to hear the holy man Shakyamuni. When he heard the name Shakyamuni, Kutadanta forgot his misgivings. The fame of this holy man was rising with the speed and brilliance of the tropical sun, not only in Magadha but throughout the Ganges plain. His reputation had reached the Brahmans, many of whom praised him, while others derided him.

Kutadanta decided that he too would go to Ambalatthika Park to ask Shakyamuni what he knew about the Grand Sacrifice. Kutadanta's disciples were astonished that their learned teacher should wish to visit the wandering monk Shakyamuni to seek instruction. "What are you saying, revered Kutadanta?" they protested. "Are you not yourself a sage, learned in the

Vedas and in contact with the gods? It is absurd that you, of the purest Brahman lineage, and honored by the king himself, should humble yourself to visit Shakyamuni. It is he who should come to you for instruction."

But Kutadanta admonished his disciples: "If we are to speak of pure lineage, the holy man Shakyamuni was the crown prince of the Shakyas. Then, gaining enlightenment, he became an omniscient sage. I have heard that the kings of Magadha, Kosala, and Malla have become his followers. Since Shakyamuni has now come to our village, I must go hear him so that I may learn for myself whether he preaches the truth." No sooner had he finished speaking than he left his mansion for the park, and his disciples hurried after him.

"This is the truth!" said Kutadanta in a voice that seemed to be wrung from deep within him. He had gone to Ambalatthika Park and heard the Buddha's teachings—teachings that were at once totally new to him, yet at the same time seemed to sum up all the religious truths he had hitherto learned. When the Buddha had finished speaking, Kutadanta went forward and prostrated himself before him. Then, taking the seat that the Buddha offered him, he began to ask about the Grand Sacrifice. The Buddha answered him with the following account of Mahavijita, an ancient king.

Long ago there lived a great king named Mahavijita. He was an excellent military leader and conquered all the neighboring kingdoms. He decided to hold a Grand Sacrifice in order to display his wealth and power and to ensure the continuing peace and well-being of his kingdom. First he consulted a Brahman in whom he had great confidence as an adviser in such matters. But the Brahman shook his head, saying, "Great king, your authority has spread throughout the land, and the kingdom seems peaceful and free from troubles. But that is only on the surface. There are many who resent you, my lord, as is evident from the continuing incidents of bloodshed and theft. If you now attempt to hold a Grand Sacrifice, levying heavy taxes to pay for it, the people will be angered and this will cause grave problems for years to come."

"How then can I lead the country to true peace?" asked the king, with some irritation.

"Great king, I suggest that instead of collecting more taxes you award special seeds and foodstuffs to those who are energetic farmers and herdsmen, and lend funds to those who have shown skill in trade. Give generous awards to officials who have performed their duties faithfully and well. If the common people are able to devote themselves to their work without distress or hindrance, they will become affluent and contented. This in turn will bring untold benefits to you and your family and ensure true peace throughout the kingdom. This method is far better than any sacrifice."

The king, persuaded by the Brahman's advice, gave up his plans for a Grand Sacrifice. And indeed, as he followed the Brahman's suggestions, he found that the common people did grow more affluent and that they were more grateful and loyal to him than ever before. Those who had vexed and troubled him in the past no longer had influence with the people. The land was truly prosperous and at peace.

Seeing how rich his kingdom had become, the king decided it was an opportune time for a sacrifice and once again consulted the Brahman. But again the Brahman responded negatively. He explained to the king in detail what conditions had to be met for a Grand Sacrifice and what the mental attitude of the sponsor must be. "In order for the gods to be truly pleased with the Grand Sacrifice, all four castes—the Brahman priests, the Kshatriya rulers and warriors, the Vaishya merchants and farmers, and the Sudra menials—should be invited to attend. If the sponsor sets up barriers among his people, he will not be able to delight the hearts of the gods, and dark clouds of calamity may overshadow your peaceful kingdom." Then the Brahman explained to the king in detail the conditions that he as sponsor of the Grand Sacrifice would have to fulfill: rectifying any misconduct on his own part, carefully controlling the armies under his command, studying the scriptures, and concentrating his thoughts on the three existences—past, present, and future. He also elucidated the sixteen rituals that the celebrant had to perform.

Mahavijita was soon able to fulfill all these conditions, but the Brahman had further advice for him: "Absolutely everyone must be invited to the Grand Sacrifice: whether guilty of taking life or not; whether guilty of robbery or not; whether guilty of lewd conduct or not; whether guilty of greed, envy, and perverse views or not. Those who are guilty of any of these sins must confess their guilt to those not guilty, and must make offerings to them; and those not guilty must pray for the deliverance of the guilty ones. When all have confessed their guilt and prayed for one

another, there will be great spiritual joy and the will to
seek the Way will arise. No sacrifice could be better
than such a ceremony of confession."

But if taking life was forbidden, it would be impossible to offer oxen, goats, sheep, and fowl in sacrifice,
or even to cut down trees or grasses for that purpose.
Pondering this problem, the king finally realized that
the Brahman was trying to tell him that he must pre-
vent the slaves from being whipped, the animals from
being cruelly sacrificed, and the trees and grasses from
being needlessly destroyed for the sake of the Grand
Sacrifice. Mahavijita felt as if scales had fallen from
his eyes. And thus he was able to conduct the Grand
Sacrifice successfully, with offerings of milk, milk
curd, oil, honey, and sugar instead of bloody victims
and severed trees and grasses.

Saying, "This was truly a Grand Sacrifice," the Buddha concluded his story with a gentle smile. Profound
joy welled up in Kutadanta as he listened, transfixed,
to the Buddha's words. He cried, "The Grand Sacrifice of King Mahavijita was a sacrifice of rare purity.
No workers slaved; no animals were killed; no trees
and grasses were mowed down. Such a sacrifice must
surely have delighted the gods!"

The Buddha nodded and continued gently: "Ah, but
in the Sangha we have a ceremony that is still purer
than the sacrifice of King Mahavijita. It is the
ceremony venerating ancestors. We offer prayers of
thanksgiving to our ancestors for having transmitted
to us the gift of life from the distant past. We make
offerings to the buddhas and transfer the merit of these
offerings to our ancestors."

Kutadanta felt happier still. "Truly," he said, "the

ceremony of making offerings for one's ancestors is an even purer sacrifice than King Mahavijita's!"

The Buddha smiled again, nodding at Kutadanta, and continued: "Friend Kutadanta, there is an even more excellent ceremony than that. It is the provision of lodgings for monks of the Sangha who wander about preaching the Dharma; it is the spirit of charitable giving, providing clothing and food for the Sangha. This can be called a spiritual offering, which far surpasses the ceremony of making offerings for one's ancestors."

Then the Buddha told Kutadanta about the merit of taking refuge in the Three Treasures—the Buddha, the Dharma, and the Sangha; the merit of arousing belief; the merit of keeping the five precepts of the lay believer and thus regulating one's daily life; the limitless merit of practicing meditation, arousing the mind to seek the Way; and the merit of benefiting others, that is, devoting oneself completely to the welfare of others. The Buddha concluded by explaining that this last practice, benefiting others, was the highest ceremony of offering, since it could lead all beings to happiness and peace.

Kutadanta was so moved he could hardly speak. Throwing himself at the Buddha's feet, he cried, "You are the sage who sees the truth of all that is! I am supposed to be learned in the Vedas, but all I know is the forms of rites and ceremonies. Now you have shown me the true meaning of rites and ceremonies, like one who reveals what has been hidden, or shows the way to one who has gone astray, or lightens the darkness. Today I take refuge in the Buddha, the Dharma, and the Sangha. Please accept me as a lay disciple."

Following their teacher's example, many young

Brahmans also asked to become lay disciples of the Buddha. Having been accepted, they returned to the village square in Khanumata to set free all the victims of the Grand Sacrifice. As the animals were led back home by their masters, they lowed and bleated and clucked happily; and the cool spring breeze of Vesakha carried the sounds far into the distance.

ISIDASI
The Bane of Three Husbands

Pataliputta, in the far north of Magadha, was a beautiful and flourishing city on the banks of the Ganges. Its quiet houses were surrounded with flowers that bloomed in turn throughout the year. One day two Buddhist nuns visited the city on their begging rounds. Both were still young, and one of them was extraordinarily graceful and attractive as she walked quietly and modestly through the streets. When they had finished begging, they went down to the partially dry bed of the Ganges, found a sandbank to sit on, and ate their lunch. As they were resting there, one nun asked the other, "Sister Isidasi, you are still young and beautiful. Tell me, why did you choose the life of a nun?"

Isidasi answered, "Well, I don't know if it will be of any use to you in your own practice, but I will be happy to tell you how I became a nun." Smiling slightly, Isidasi began her story.

Like you, I belong to the Shakya tribe. My father went into business in Ujjeni, the capital of Avanti, and was very successful. I was an only child, and my parents showered me with affection. When I was happy, they were; if I was troubled for any reason, however trifling, they did everything they could to cheer me up. I was never criticized by anyone for anything. Our many servants praised me constantly, saying that everything I did was perfect. When I reached marriageable age, my parents made great efforts to find a suitable husband for me. "Isidasi," they would say, "there's no girl on earth as clever, attractive, and good natured as you. We'll find you a splendid match so that your married life will be as happy as you deserve."

Time and again my parents made comments like this. One day they received a marriage proposal that seemed to fulfill all their hopes. A messenger came from one of the first families of the city of Saketa, in Kosala, to ask for my hand on behalf of his master's son, who was not only immensely rich but also reportedly very handsome. "A perfect match for our daughter!" cried my parents happily, and soon everything was settled.

On a bright, sunny day that seemed like a blessing from the gods, I set off for Saketa, dressed in bridal finery and seen off by a throng of well-wishers. From the day I entered my new family, I worked hard to perform my duties as a wife to perfection. Morning and evening I visited my parents-in-law in their rooms and greeted them respectfully, prostrating myself before them so that my head touched their feet. Whenever one of my husband's relatives entered a room I was in, I gave him or her my seat and took a lower one for myself. In the morning I got up earlier than anyone else and made breakfast for the family. I tried to prepare delicacies each person would enjoy. Then I would go to my husband's room to wake him. After washing my hands and feet at the entrance, I would comb his hair and help him dress, as careful and respectful as any servant.

I was doing just as my parents had instructed me to do before my marriage. "When you marry," they had said, "you must serve your husband with all your strength. A bride must be humble toward everyone, rise before anyone else, and never allow herself to fall into idleness or sloth." I had confidence in my own abilities, and my new parents-in-law, observing me act in accordance with the traditional precepts, exclaimed in admiration, "My, what a wonderful bride!" But for some reason, the harder I worked to be a perfect wife, the more dissatisfied my husband seemed to become. "You don't have to do that, you know," he would say to me from time to time, and I would answer, "But this is my duty as your wife."

Eventually, though, my husband came to dislike my wifely attentions so much that he would shout angrily at me. Then one day he said something that stunned me: "I can't stand another day of living with that woman Isidasi! Father, Mother, please, I want your permission to divorce her." His parents were amazed at this outburst and asked what he could find to complain of in a wife as clever and diligent as I. He answered, "She is indeed a perfect wife. But even so, I don't love her, and that's that. In fact, I dislike her. If you won't approve a divorce, I'll just have to leave the family myself."

No matter what his parents said, he remained adamant. Finally they came to me and asked, "What did you do? Did you slight him or rebuke him?" I just shook my head. My parents-in-law were distressed,

but there was nothing they could do but follow their
son's wishes in the matter. When my father-in-law
took me back to my family's home in Ujjeni, he looked
up to heaven sorrowfully and said, "Surely we must
have been abandoned by the goddess of good fortune,
to have such a thing happen."

I told myself that my former husband was simply incapable of appreciating me. My father insisted I was
"too good for the likes of him" and that he would find
me a more suitable husband. Very soon he found a can-
didate: the family was a little lower in status than my
first husband's but still well-to-do, and the son was
said to be a kind young man.

"They're of lower status than my own family, so I'm
sure my new husband will show me respect and
recognize my real worth," I thought. Off I went, taking along about half the valuables I had taken to my
first husband's family as my dowry. I worked even
harder than before at being a model wife. I served my
husband and in-laws until I was worn to a frazzle. I
was sure no one would be able to criticize me and that
everything would be all right this time.

Then one day, out of the blue, my husband shouted,
"I can't stand it anymore! Go back to your own family!
I want you out of my house!" I felt as if I had been
struck by lightning. "He's just the same as my first
husband. Why must I end up with people like this?" I
thought. Once again sent back to my father's house, I
was overcome with chagrin and embarrassment and
shut myself up in my room for some time.

My parents, too, must have felt terrible about what
had happened. They said there was no need for me to
grieve so, that they knew I had done nothing to be
ashamed of. I had just been unlucky in my marriage

partners. Now they would find a man of real character for me. It was not status or money that mattered but character.

The person my father chose as my third husband was a man of religion, known for his ability to control himself and influence others thanks to his long years of religious training and mendicancy. He had come to our door one day on his begging rounds, and my parents, hoping I would find happiness at last, had persuaded him to marry me. They must have moved him to sympathy by their pleas. He put aside his robe and begging bowl and became my third husband.

I served him faithfully, this man with the calm, deep gaze that seemed to penetrate everything around him. Quietly, gently, he observed me. And then one day he went to my parents and said, "I want to take up my robe and bowl again. I want to resume my life as a man of religion."

"Is there something that does not meet with your approval in our household? If there's something you want changed, just say so. We'll do anything you want," my father replied anxiously.

"The only thing I want is freedom to live alone, apart from Isidasi. I need nothing else."

I stood there dumbfounded. If only I had had some hint of what was wrong, I could have tried to do something about it. But I just could not imagine what might be wrong. I felt as if I had been rejected by the whole world, cast aside by everyone.

After my third husband left, I spent more and more time in lonely thought. I wanted to leave home, but where was I to go? There seemed no place for me but the land of the dead. When I had almost decided to kill myself, Sister Jinadatta came to our house on her begging rounds. She seemed to have a certain nobility about her. Drawn as if against my will, I knelt before her, bowed, and said, "Reverend sister, please help me become a nun. I wish to enter the Sangha above all else."

Sister Jinadatta looked at me steadily. My father, who was sitting nearby, said, "Isidasi, you can follow the teachings of the Buddha and make offerings to the monks while remaining here at home with us." I pressed my palms together respectfully and begged my father's permission. The words seemed to tumble forth of their own accord: "I've gone on creating bad karma for myself, both in this world and in the next. And because of my sinfulness I've injured three husbands in succession. I must somehow do penance for these sins."

At last, hearing my own words, I understood: it was myself I loved. If I worked my fingers to the bone, it was to gain a sense of self-satisfaction. I had been told from childhood how fine I was, and I had believed it. As a result, I had never tried to understand my husbands as people who needed love. Day after day I had offended them without even being aware of it.

Without stopping to wipe away my tears, I turned to my parents and asked their permission to become a nun. They smiled and nodded, saying they hoped I would seek the highest truth and find peace.

And so I left the secular world, saying farewell to my father and mother, my relatives, and the servants, and earnestly sought the truth. Gradually I began to be aware of what I had been, was now, and would probably become. It was terrifying. I thought I had committed no sin, but in fact I had injured many people. If I had not been able to enter the religious life, no doubt

I would have fallen into the depths of hell without ever realizing my own guilt. Now I know from my own experience how broad and deep the compassion of the Buddha truly is.

When Isidasi's long tale was finished, the sun was setting in the west. The Ganges spread out before the two nuns, its broad waters reddened by the evening light. Quietly they began to wend their way back to their convent, each lost in her own thoughts.

SUNITA
The Night-Soil Carrier

"Why do I have to do this filthy work day after day? Why must I be hated and despised by everyone?" thought Sunita resentfully. He had been born a Sudra, a member of the lowest caste, and earned his living by going from house to house, collecting night soil and disposing of it on the outskirts of the city. His body was permeated by the smell, and the townspeople held their noses and made faces when they saw him.

Sunita could not escape this contemptuous treatment because there was no other work for him to do, and he had no relatives to help him better himself. He fell into despair and stopped caring about himself: he let his hair grow long and matted, wore his clothes until they hung from him in rags, and never troubled to wash.

One morning Sunita set off as usual on his rounds of the houses in Savatthi, the capital of the kingdom of Kosala. Just outside the city was the Jetavana Monastery, where Shakyamuni was staying. As Sunita entered a street on the outskirts of the city, he heard an excited clamor: "The Buddha's here!" "Let's go pay him reverence!"

Curious, Sunita ran behind the crowd. Suddenly he saw a man moving slowly in his direction. Everyone around this man was bowing, palms pressed together in reverence. It was the Buddha, coming to receive alms in Savatthi. "How wise and holy he looks," thought Sunita. "His body seems to shine like the sun." He felt as if he had shrunk to nothing before the stately figure of the Buddha.

Just then a man who was trying to slip past Sunita to get closer to the Buddha happened to bump into Sunita and cried out, "What an awful stench! What do you think you're doing, loitering here! Off with you!" Startled by the man's angry shouts, the bystanders all stared at Sunita, who suddenly became aware that he was still carrying a jar of night soil on his back. He cringed before the cold stares of the crowd, then noticed with a start that the Buddha's gaze, too, was directed toward him. Sunita was overcome with shame. His face aflame with embarrassment, he ran into an alley.

He wondered, "Why was I born a Sudra, forced to spend my life doing work like this? Everyone else goes forward to revere the Buddha, but I can't!" Having seen how pure the Buddha was, Sunita could no longer remain indifferent to his own filthiness. Hiding in the narrow alley, he sobbed like a child, cursing his fate. Suddenly he became aware of someone's presence. Raising his head, he was stunned to see the Buddha moving slowly toward him.

Sunita was thunderstruck. "How is it that the Buddha is walking here, in this alley?" He began to back up as fast as he could. He thought, "The Buddha fills this town with the fragrance of his pure spirit, but I fill it with the stench of excrement. If I come close to the Buddha, I will defile his purity."

Sunita hurried into a still narrower alley. He ran for a bit, then stopped, panting for breath. To his amazement, he saw the Buddha again, standing a little way ahead of him. "I can't go this way! The Buddha is the holiest being in this world. And me, I'm the lowest of the low. If I dared approach the Buddha, the gods would strike me dead!"

Sunita hunted frantically for an escape. Yet wherever he went, he saw the Buddha standing in front of him. He did not know what to do.

By now Sunita's body was so stiff with embarrassment that it would not do as he wished. Summoning up his last reserve of strength, he twisted his body to avoid the Buddha. In doing so, he bumped against an earthen wall, lost his balance, and tumbled to the ground. Unfortunately, the large jar he was carrying on his back also fell and broke, spreading its unsavory contents over the ground. And in the middle of the pool of excrement sat Sunita, covered with filth from head to foot. Unable to breathe because of the stench, his face ashen, Sunita found himself trembling uncontrollably. He tried desperately to stand up but slipped and fell back into the muck. "I wish I could die and be done with it!" he thought in despair. He sat on the ground in the filth, having lost even the will to run away. Bowing his head till it almost touched the ground, he pressed his palms together and moaned, "Please, I beg you, move aside a little so I can go. I'm so filthy."

Crouched on the ground, wishing he could die, Sunita was aware of the presence of someone very near. Looking up, he saw the Buddha bending over him with a gentle smile. "Sunita, Sunita." The voice seemed gently to enfold him. But Sunita shook his head in disbelief. How could the Buddha, before whom even kings and rich men prostrated themselves, be calling *his* name? He could not believe his ears. Yet there was no one else nearby. Sunita sat on the ground stunned. Then the Buddha addressed him again: "Sunita, it is for your sake that I have come. There is within you a pure, fragrant, and radiant spirit. Do not despise yourself. Where would you flee to avoid me, who has come for your sake?"

Despite himself, Sunita raised his eyes and looked at the Buddha; and as he did, a mysterious power welled up within him. He thought, "I have no parents, no family or relatives. I work all day in filth, like an animal or a hungry ghost. And yet when I hear your voice I feel as if I were being cleansed, both outwardly and inwardly."

A sudden resolve formed in Sunita's mind: he would engrave the memory of this noble, pure, incomparably beautiful man's form and voice on his heart. He would never forget him. At that moment, the Buddha spoke again to the amazed Sunita: "Come, follow me. Enter my brotherhood, the Sangha, and become a monk."

"Me? You mean someone like me can become your disciple?"

"Sunita, the enlightenment that I have attained is precisely for the poor, for those who suffer, for those who know their own unworthiness and lament it. The Dharma I preach is like a pure river from which all can drink—the rich and the poor, kings and outcasts. Through it, all can attain nirvana. Believe my words, Sunita, and come, follow me."

Sunita thought, "I was born a miserable Sudra and have been poor and hungry all my life. Eventually I became base in mind and spirit, too. Covered with filth, I have been hated, rebuked, and scorned by everyone. Now the Buddha has accepted me as one of his disciples, as one who seeks the Way that leads to the highest enlightenment. If, after all this, I should weaken in my resolve to seek the Way, surely I would fall into the lowest hell."

So Sunita exerted himself day after day, living alone in the depths of the forest and practicing in accordance with the Buddha's teachings. One night, after a long period of intensive meditation, the veil of ignorance was finally lifted and all Sunita's mental defilements vanished.

Shortly thereafter, it came to the ears of King Pasenadi in Savatthi that the Buddha had permitted the Sudra Sunita to join the Sangha. The king thought, "The Sangha should be an assembly of the purest, noblest people. Why did the Buddha admit this Sudra, a night-soil carrier? When the Buddha and his disciples come to my palace, even I, the king, prostrate myself and pay reverence at their feet. Am I then to prostrate myself before a lowly Sudra? I must ask the Buddha himself about this."

Pasenadi immediately readied his carriage and set off for the Jetavana Monastery. When he arrived at the gate, he saw a monk sitting on a large rock nearby, mending his robe. To his amazement, Pasenadi saw a throng of heavenly beings surrounding the monk, their palms pressed together in reverence. Pasenadi got down from his carriage, bowed with great respect, and addressed the monk: "I am Pasenadi, the king of this land. Would you be kind enough to tell the Buddha that I have come to seek an audience with him?"

But indeed this was no ordinary monk, for no sooner had he heard the king's words than he bowed and disappeared within the rock. A short time later, he emerged from it and beckoned the startled monarch to enter the monastery. Entering Shakyamuni's presence, King Pasenadi addressed him: "I have come today to ask the Buddha about his having admitted the Sudra Sunita to the Sangha. But first I should like to ask the Buddha about the venerable monk who guided me here. I found him attended by a company of heavenly beings; then he entered and emerged from a rock as if it were water—I saw these marvels with my own eyes!"

The Buddha listened quietly to Pasenadi and then replied, "Your Majesty, the monk who guided you here is none other than Sunita, about whom you came to inquire. You can see that even a Sudra, who must handle things that are unclean, can attain such mystical powers if he applies himself earnestly to religious practice, just as the lotus, emerging from the mud at the bottom of a pool, bears beautiful flowers, red and blue and white. Thus, one must not judge people by their birth. Rather, one should consider what they have within them."

At these words King Pasenadi profoundly repented his pride and prostrated himself, paying reverence to the Buddha and to his disciple Sunita the Sudra.

BHADDA
The Robber's Wife

Rajagaha, the capital of Magadha, was abuzz with rumors. The young robber chieftain Satthuka, who had recently been captured, was being paraded around the city, bound hand and foot and tied to the back of an old nag. People lined the streets, eager to catch a glimpse of the notorious robber whose life was about to end. Cries of derision, and a few murmurs of pity, rose from the crowd.

Satthuka's horse passed in front of a certain rich man's house. Hearing the clamor outside, the rich man's only daughter, Bhadda, rushed to the balcony off her bedroom and gazed down at the street. At precisely that moment Satthuka looked up at her, his eyes filled with pain and fear. Bhadda leaned forward in surprise. "He's far too handsome for a robber!" she thought. Bhadda was pierced to the heart by those large, dark eyes appealing to her desperately for help. It was said that he had terrorized the city, but she knew he could not have done such wicked things on his own. He must have been misled by somebody. She was sure his heart was pure. She decided to save him.

Bhadda was both clever and beautiful, and her

parents loved her more than anything in the world. "Well, if it's what she wants," they would say, and Bhadda would get her way. This was how she had been reared, and as a result she was very willful.

Bhadda rushed to her father's room and begged him, "Father, please save Satthuka's life. He's not really a bad man. I couldn't bear to go on living if we let him die!" Her father, taken aback, tried every argument to induce Bhadda to change her mind. But she was as stubborn as always, and her indulgent father could deny her nothing. Besides, he had confidence in her intelligence and judgment.

Though realizing that Bhadda's pity for the handsome young robber chieftain was not unmixed with passionate longing, her father gathered together a large sum in gold and bribed the prison guards. That night, as the city slept, Satthuka was spirited out of prison.

Meanwhile, Bhadda was waiting in her room, her heart aflutter with expectancy. The whole room, and especially the bed, was festooned with sumptuous decorations. Bhadda herself was scented with fine perfumes and wore a diaphanous gown glittering with gems. When the servants conducted Satthuka to Bhadda's room, she welcomed him warmly, her body trembling with joy and excitement. At first Satthuka just smiled vaguely in bewilderment at all that had happened; but when he noticed Bhadda's jewels, his eyes began to glitter, though Bhadda was too entranced to notice. That very night the two young people exchanged vows of marriage and consummated their union. Bhadda's dreams were the sweetest she had ever known.

A few days later, Satthuka said with a serious air,

"Bhadda, it was at a spot called Robbers' Cliff, half-way up the mountain a little way out of Rajagaha, that I was captured. The god of the place is enshrined on the mountain. When they caught me, I prayed, 'I know my luck has run out. But if you'll only save me this one last time, I promise I'll give up this evil trade and bring rich offerings here in thanksgiving.' Well, I was saved, and was lucky enough to become your husband. I must go offer thanks at the shrine, and you should go with me. I want you to wear the beautiful gown you had on the night we met. And put on all those jewels, too."

"Of course," replied Bhadda. "I'll just have the servants prepare the offerings, and we can be off." Cheerfully she began to prepare for the pilgrimage. Satthuka's insistence on fulfilling his vow seemed to her proof that she had been right about him.

Bhadda and Satthuka started off for Robbers' Cliff with a great crowd of attendants. The bystanders never dreamed that the elegant young gentleman who accompanied Bhadda was the robber chieftain Satthuka. When the party reached a grove a short distance from Robbers' Cliff, Satthuka stopped the carriage and announced that he and Bhadda would have to proceed alone, since they were entering holy ground. A shadow of uneasiness momentarily passed over Bhadda's heart, but in obedience to her husband's words she left the attendants and climbed the mountain alone with him. When they reached the top, Bhadda found her legs trembling and her heart pounding as she looked down from the dizzying height. Controlling her fear, she said, "Let's hurry and say our prayers of thanksgiving. Where shall I put these offerings?"

But Satthuka's attitude was transformed. "Oh, Bhadda," he said with a derisive laugh, "do you really think I came here to make offerings to some god? What a little fool you are! Listen carefully. I brought you here today so I could take those jewels from your pretty little body and then send you to heaven via this cliff. Understand?" He concluded with another mocking laugh.

Bhadda felt numb. Everything she had believed was false. Her head began to swim; she was in total confusion. Then Satthuka moved to grab her. "You're joking, you *must* be! These jewels and everything I have are yours!" cried Bhadda. But the robber chieftain, closing in on his prey, did not seem to hear. He came toward her with murder in his eyes. Behind her was a precipice. There seemed no escape. Bhadda's instinct for self-preservation prompted her to stammer, "If you want these jewels so much, I'll give them all to you. And if you want my life, you can have that, too. I can't stop loving you. I don't care about anything else, but I want you to hold me in your arms one last time before I die."

Delighted with Bhadda's meek attitude, Satthuka smiled indulgently and approached her with open arms. Suddenly Bhadda pushed at his unprotected chest, and Satthuka, losing his footing, plunged headlong over the cliff. Bhadda stood quite still for a time. She could not believe what had happened. The sun began to sink in the western sky, and she slowly came to herself. She went to where her attendants were waiting and told them, "We'll be coming back later. You are to return home by yourselves, at once." Bhadda felt she could not go back to the house where she had exchanged vows with Satthuka.

"I have no desire to remain in this vain, deceitful world," she sighed to herself. Shaking her head in sorrow and disgust at her own folly, she wandered aimlessly along the steadily darkening path. Happening to encounter a band of Jain ascetics, she joined them. In accordance with the severe rules governing this sect, she tore out her long black hair by the roots with a rough comb made of palm wood.

Bhadda devoted herself to severe ascetic practice from that day on. Yet no matter how much she punished her body, she could find no peace of mind. She embarked on a long pilgrimage, visiting spiritual masters in various towns and villages. Even so, she could not find a teacher in whom she was fully confident. Most of the Brahmans themselves were quite intimidated by Bhadda's formidable powers of debate.

Bhadda's hair, which had been torn out by the roots, had grown back in the form of kinky stubble. People were repelled by her looks, calling her Bhadda-Kundalakesa, or Stubble-haired Bhadda, and keeping their distance from her. But she did not seem to notice; her only concern was to find a master who would help her attain peace of mind.

In the course of her quest she traveled to distant Savatthi, the capital of Kosala. Savatthi was one of the greatest cities of India, along with Rajagaha, where Bhadda had been born. Arriving at the great gate of the city, she stuck a branch of a *jambu* tree upright into the ground beside it to indicate her willingness to debate any local teacher who wished to accept the challenge. Telling the children who were playing by the gate to inform anyone who wished to debate her to bend the branch as a sign, she went into the city to beg her daily food. But there were few who would accept her challenge, since Stubble-haired Bhadda's skill in debate was widely known.

One day, however, when Bhadda returned from her begging rounds, she found the *jambu* branch bent and a monk seated deep in meditation nearby. He was none other than Sariputta, known as the wisest of all the disciples of the Buddha. He had come to Savatthi that day, seen the *jambu* branch, heard the children's report, and immediately divined what Bhadda was seeking.

The debate between the two was held there, by the city gate, before a great crowd of onlookers. First Bhadda posed questions for Sariputta to answer. She asked the hardest questions she could think of and was stunned to hear Sariputta answer each with ease. "This is no ordinary mendicant," she said to herself as she exhausted her repertoire of difficult questions.

Then it was Sariputta's turn. "I have only one question for you, Bhadda," he said. "What is the One?"

Bhadda was at a loss to reply. The question seemed at first childishly simple, but she could not get to the heart of it. As she struggled with the problem, she began gradually to realize that Sariputta was not her opponent in debate but her mentor. "Please tell me the answer to your question," she implored.

"I would answer that the One is equivalent to all things; and all things return to the One. Now then, Bhadda, do you think that someone who cannot answer such a basic question can understand more complex matters?" Then, without a backward glance, Sariputta withdrew. His last words had pierced Bhadda's soul like a knife. She hurried after him and begged to be allowed to become his disciple. Sariputta replied, "I only transmit what I have learned from my teacher, Shakyamuni. If you wish to be accepted as a disciple, you must make your request to him." And he guided her to the Jetavana Monastery.

The Buddha spoke to Bhadda as she lay prostrate on the ground before him: "Open your eyes and you will see that all things in this world are impure, impermanent, and full of sorrow. And they are all lacking in any real substance. Bhadda, even if you should know a thousand verses of scripture by heart, if your mind is not at peace you cannot be compared with one who has peace of mind, though that person knows only a fraction of one verse."

Bhadda realized that at last she had found the teacher she had been seeking. She became a member of the Sangha, having taken refuge in the Buddha, the Dharma, and the Sangha, and spent the remaining fifty years of her life in zealous pursuit of the Way. She traveled through the lands of Anga, Magadha, the Vajji confederation, Malla, Kasi, and Kosala, preaching the Dharma and winning fame as the nun quickest in apprehending truth.

SUNDARINANDA
The Nun Trapped by Her Beauty

Sundarinanda was the Buddha's half sister, a daughter of Mahapajapati, who was the second wife of Shakyamuni's father, King Suddhodana. There were four princesses, but Sundarinanda was by far the most beautiful. As a child, she had become used to people making a fuss over her. She was treated as a person of consequence, and her every need was seen to by others. All this she came to regard as no more than her due. She knew also that the people referred to her as the most beautiful woman in the land of the Shakyas.

A great change occurred in Sundarinanda's life after the death of her father, King Suddhodana. As soon as the prescribed period of mourning had ended, her mother, Mahapajapati, requested and was given permission by the Buddha to enter the Sangha. Then Yasodhara, the Buddha's former wife, also left the palace to become a nun.

The four princesses remembered how their older half brother, Prince Siddhattha, had given up his riches and status to enter the religious life and become the Buddha. His only son, Rahula, and their older brother, Nanda, had done likewise. Now their mother and Princess Yasodhara had left the palace to become nuns. Day after day the four princesses talked over what they would do if left there by themselves, until finally they decided to become nuns, as well. Sundarinanda thought, "If I become a nun, I can be with Mother and my older brother every day. They've always loved me and taken care of me—it'll be wonderful!"

And so the four sisters set out together for the Jetavana Monastery, outside Savatthi, the capital of distant Kosala, and asked the Buddha's permission to enter the Sangha. Approval was readily given, but the life of a nun proved to be more difficult than they had imagined. A nun must abandon the use of all costly garments, ornaments, and cosmetics; she wears the simplest robes and does all tasks on her own, without the help of servants, working from dawn to late night. And she must be careful to show respect to every nun who is senior to her in the Sangha.

"What a confined, unpleasant, inconvenient life this is!" Such complaints were often on Sundarinanda's lips, since she had left her comfortable life in the palace without a sincere desire to seek the Way. Aware of the eyes of the monks, nuns, and laymen who were impressed by her beauty, she behaved as if she were still a princess living in a palace.

The Buddha often had occasion to admonish her, saying, "Sundarinanda, are you still possessed by pride in your own beauty? Can you not cast away that pride, now that you have renounced the world?" After being scolded like this several times, Sundarinanda began to avoid the Buddha altogether.

Eventually, though, she began to reflect on her conduct and attempted to practice in strict accordance with the Buddha's teaching. But when, on her begging rounds, she felt the admiring gaze of laymen upon her, she would unconsciously drift back to her old frame of mind. Then, when she realized what was happening and tried to avoid contact with such people, the Buddha would again reprove her, saying, "Sundarinanda, do you have improper feelings toward the laymen who make offerings? If not, you should be able to accept offerings from everyone without discrimination, in the spirit of selflessness."

Poor Sundarinanda felt like crying. She thought, "It's not *my* fault I was born beautiful. The people who make such a fuss about it are the ones to blame. But *I'm* the one who gets scolded. What can I do?" She did not realize that the Buddha was trying to teach her that precisely because of her great beauty she would have to behave even more modestly, humbly, and purely than others if she wished to attain happiness.

Though she tried to devote herself to religious practices that would lead to greater self-knowledge and self-control, it was very difficult for her, reared in a palace and pampered all her life, to control her desires. In fact, the life of a nun had become distasteful to her. "Why should I spend the precious days of my youth in this dreary way of life?" Such thoughts occurred to her often.

It was at about this time that a young man named Salha, a grandson of the female lay disciple Visakha, requested that he be allowed to build a convent for the growing number of nuns. The Buddha accepted Salha's offer and chose the clever young nun Sundarinanda to supervise its construction. When Salha went to the monastery for the first time to discuss the progress of the work with Sundarinanda, he was immediately infatuated with her. Salha was an extremely handsome youth, and the nun felt her heart flutter at the sight of him. And so it happened that Salha began to visit the monastery almost daily. The more he saw of the young nun, the more attractive she seemed. Waking or sleeping, he could not keep her out of his thoughts.

Salha hit on a plan that would enable him to confess his love to Sundarinanda. He decided to invite all the nuns of the Sangha to his house for a feast and devise an excuse to see Sundarinanda alone on that occasion. Sundarinanda knew precisely what it was Salha was trying to do, and her heart was torn. Hard though it was, she resolved not to attend the feast. When the day came, she complained of not feeling well and remained in the monastery. No sooner was she alone, though, than she began to feel sorry for Salha, who obviously cared for her deeply. She realized that her pity for him sprang from love and was ashamed of her violation of the spirit of her vows; yet she could not help herself. Gazing at the distant lights of the city, she thought of Salha. Then, to her amazement, she caught a glimpse of someone climbing the path that led from the city to the monastery. It was none other than Salha. Trembling, Sundarinanda burrowed into her bedclothes, pulled the blanket up over her head, and held her breath. Whom did she fear—Salha or herself?

The monastery was completely silent, but Salha, being familiar with the layout, found his way in. He was surprised to find the young nun hiding under a blanket and asked her what was wrong. There was no reply. He slowly pulled the blanket from her. Seeing her flushed face, he exclaimed, "Why, you have a fever!"

Then Sundarinanda said something that amazed them both: "How else could I feel when I meet the man I love, even though he doesn't love me!" The words spilled out of their own accord; it was too late to take them back.

"The man you love . . . could that possibly be me? If so, how can you say I don't love you? It's just that I've had no chance to tell you how I feel!" As he spoke, Salha took Sundarinanda's hand and stepped closer to her. Sundarinanda could no longer control herself; she clasped his hand and buried her face in his chest. The warning voice of reason grew weaker and more distant, and finally Sundarinanda surrendered to her passion.

Unknown to the lovers, there remained in the monastery one aged nun, crippled by a bad leg. There was nothing wrong with either her ears or her tongue, however, and the lovers' secret was soon common knowledge throughout the monastery. Soon after, the Buddha summoned Sundarinanda. She was in great confusion, overcome with self-loathing.

Gazing at her steadily, the Buddha bade her sit beside him and guided her into a profound meditative trance. She saw the figure of an extraordinarily beautiful young woman. As she fixed her attention on the lovely form, however, it began to change: it grew old and ugly, fell to the ground, and rotted away before Sundarinanda's eyes. Terrified, she began to tremble and emerged abruptly from her trance. Then the Buddha spoke to her gently, saying, "You see, Sundarinanda, how even a maiden of flowerlike beauty must inevitably grow old and lose her looks; how she must suffer the pangs of illness and finally encounter death and corruption. Only the foolish would attach themselves to such a frail, corruptible thing as the body, and plunge themselves into the ocean of sorrow for the sake of fleeting pleasures and momentary glory. Therefore, Sundarinanda, you must always reflect on the impure nature of the physical body and earnestly continue to seek the realm of absolute peace and eternal joy. From today on, devote yourself totally to the practices that can free you from physical desire and all selfish attachments."

Each word seemed to pierce Sundarinanda's heart. It was as if the Buddha's words were exorcising the passions that lurked within her. Clenching her teeth, she admonished herself: "Because of my physical beauty, I have been subject to temptations from those who have been attracted to me, and thus have fallen into evil ways. I should have left all that behind me when I became a nun, but instead I have continued to take pride in my looks and so have injured many people. Unless I free myself from these bonds, I will surely continue to inflict injury on others and suffering on myself."

As soon as she had come to this clear realization about herself, it was as if Sundarinanda had been reborn. She devoted herself to the Meditation on the Body's Impurities. Ultimately she was able to attain a state of perfect indifference toward her previously prized and pampered body. Thus freed from all self-attachment, Sundarinanda attained the enlightenment of an *arahant,* abiding in a state of constant peace.

BHADDIYA
The King Who Became a Monk

Some distance east of Rajagaha, the capital of Magadha, lay Champa, the capital of Anga. Shakyamuni, accompanied by many disciples, happened to be visiting Champa. One night the disciples were immersed in meditation in a forest on the outskirts of the city. Not a sound could be heard, until suddenly the stillness was broken by a cry: "Ah, how pleasant! What a wonderful feeling!"

The monks, seated in meditation under trees or on great rocks, were startled and upset by the sound. It was repeated: "Ah, how pleasant! What a wonderful feeling!" They wondered who was crazy enough to shout like that in the middle of a meditation session. They stopped meditating and moved toward the voice. There they discovered the monk Bhaddiya, deep in meditation, to be sure, but uttering cries of delight as he sat there.

Bhaddiya's noble features revealed his aristocratic birth. In fact, he was related to Shakyamuni's father, King Suddhodana, and had become king of the Shakyas after Suddhodana's death. When the other monks realized that the cries that had disturbed them came from Bhaddiya, they nodded to one another with disgusted looks on their faces.

Bhaddiya had been severely reprimanded by the Buddha shortly after his entry into the Sangha because he had failed to show the respect due to the monk Upali as his senior. Upali, also from the Shakya kingdom, had served as court barber before becoming a monk. In ancient India, the occupation of barber was considered base; it was unthinkable for someone like Upali to share a meal with a man of royal blood or even to converse with him. However, Upali had accompanied Bhaddiya and five other young Shakya nobles and had asked to join the Sangha at the same time. The Buddha had admitted them all, but had ordained Upali first. According to the rules of the Sangha, a person ordained one day, or even one minute, before another was regarded as the other's senior and was to be greeted with a respectful bow.

But it was hard for Bhaddiya, who had been a king, to regard the lowly Upali as being on the same level as himself, much less his superior. The idea of bowing respectfully to Upali the barber seemed absurd. When the Buddha noticed this attitude, he rebuked Bhaddiya, saying, "Why do you neglect to pay respect to Upali as your senior in the Sangha?"

Bhaddiya replied indignantly, "Upali may be my senior in the Sangha, but he is of mean birth, while I, like you, am a member of the royal house. Formerly he was my servant. How can I bow to him? It would dishonor the royal house of the Shakyas!"

"I understand, Bhaddiya," said the Buddha. "I too once felt pride in belonging to the Shakya royal house. But remember this: even though you were born into a rich and noble family and Upali into a poor one of low caste, both of you will experience sickness and old age; both of you will inevitably be brought into contact with those you dislike and separated from those you love. In the teaching of the buddhas all are equal, whether they are of noble birth or humble, whether they are dressed in fine robes or in rags. And that is why you must pay respect to Upali as one who is senior to you in the Sangha, even if only by a little.''

The Buddha's words seemed to awaken Bhaddiya from a deep sleep. But many of the monks who heard the exchange between Bhaddiya and the Buddha received the impression that Bhaddiya was arrogant, priding himself on his high birth. Every time they caught sight of his noble features their antipathy grew. They considered his crying out during meditation outrageous. Apparently Bhaddiya had enjoyed himself in every conceivable way when he was in the royal palace; now—they thought—he recalled his former pleasures during the meditation period. How shameful this was in one who was supposed to be developing an awareness of the suffering inherent in all existence! The monks' resentment grew as they gossiped among themselves.

Indeed, it was true that Bhaddiya had lived a life of pleasure in the palace in the Shakya capital of Kapila-vatthu, guarded by soldiers and served by beautiful attendants. One bright moonlit night he was playing the cithern, surrounded by his ladies-in-waiting, when suddenly a string broke with a loud twang. Just then, a visitor arrived; it was his cousin Anuruddha.

"Your Majesty," he began, with a look of firm resolve on his face, "the young men of this land vie with one another to be the first to enter the Sangha, drawn by the fame of Shakyamuni, who recently visited Kapilavatthu. I too have resolved to enter the Sangha, but my mother has refused to give me her permission. She will allow it only on the condition that you, our king, also become a monk. Won't you join me in entering the religious life under the Buddha?"

Bhaddiya was overwhelmed by Anuruddha's fervor. He also began to feel an unbearable loneliness. He thought, "So Anuruddha has decided to join the Sangha, too. I'll be the only one left behind." And so Bhaddiya decided to speak to his mother. "Ours is the only family in the royal house of the Shakyas that has yet to produce a member of the Sangha. Please, Mother, give me your permission to become a monk," he begged.

Bhaddiya's mother loved him so much that she was unwilling to let him out of her sight for more than a few moments at a time. She was not about to allow him to leave the palace and live as a wandering mendicant. But Bhaddiya was determined, and insisted that she give him permission to join the Sangha. Finally, thinking it her last chance to keep him from carrying out his resolve, his mother answered, "Well, if Anuruddha's mother consents to his becoming a monk, then I will also give my permission." She assumed that Anuruddha's mother would never permit her beloved son to take such a step. Bhaddiya was overjoyed at his mother's words.

When Anuruddha heard the news, he proposed that the two of them set off immediately to enter the Sangha. But Bhaddiya suddenly felt uneasy. "Once I become a monk, it'll be goodbye forever to the palace life," he thought. "We're still young. There's plenty of time for us to enjoy ourselves a little longer and *then* become monks." Such were his thoughts; his words to Anuruddha differed somewhat: "We have certain duties and responsibilities as members of the royal house. We must make sure things go smoothly for others after we're gone. Why don't we put off becoming monks for a while and make careful preparations—say, for about seven years?"

Anuruddha would not hear of such a thing. "How can you say that? Hasn't the Buddha taught us the impermanent nature of this world, that in this world of dew we know neither the day nor the hour of our death? Why, we may be dead long before your seven years are up!"

"Well, what about five years?"

"That's absurd!"

"Three years might be . . ."

"No!"

Bhaddiya suggested shorter and shorter waiting periods, but Anuruddha was adamant. At last they agreed on a seven-day postponement. On the day appointed, they left Kapilavatthu with four other young men of noble birth—Ananda, Bhagu, Devadatta, and Kimbila—and set out for the town of Anupiya in the neighboring state of Malla, where Shakyamuni was staying. Accompanying them was the court barber, Upali.

When the six noble youths stood before the Buddha and requested admission to the Sangha, he spoke first to Upali: "Do you also wish to join the Sangha, Upali?"

"Yes, but I am a Sudra, a member of the lowest caste. Can someone like me gain admission to the Sangha?"

"According to the Dharma, there is no distinction between young and old, high and low, rich and poor.

Anyone who takes refuge in the Three Treasures, keeps the precepts, and sincerely practices the teachings can enter the Sangha," replied the Buddha with a gentle smile. He then administered the precepts to Upali before any of the others.

By ordaining Upali first and thus making him senior to the others, the Buddha was trying to teach the young Shakya nobles that they must cut off all attachment to their former worldly status. This was a particularly difficult task for Bhaddiya. Nevertheless, when the Buddha admonished him and taught him the importance of showing respect to Upali, he experienced an awakening. "The most important part of religious training is the conquest of one's pride," he thought. "If I continue to be concerned about my former position and indulge in longing for my old life in the palace, I'll never be able to attain enlightenment."

Having been born to royal rank, Bhaddiya had never before been reprimanded by anyone. The Buddha's words thus came as a great shock, and through this experience Bhaddiya began to understand the inner meaning of becoming a monk. For the first time he glimpsed the path to true egolessness. Unfortunately, his fellow monks could not observe this inner transformation. They continued to regard him as an arrogant monk who took great pride in his royal birth.

The morning after the incident in the forest, the monks went to the Buddha as a group and reported Bhaddiya's conduct the previous night. Summoned by the Buddha, Bhaddiya prostrated himself. Then, taking the seat indicated, he awaited the Buddha's questions.

"Bhaddiya, I have heard that you cried out, 'Ah,

how pleasant! What a wonderful feeling!' as you sat in meditation in the forest last night. Is this so?"

"It is so."

"And why did you cry out those words, Bhaddiya?"

The monk pressed his palms together and answered respectfully: "Please let me explain. When I was king of the Shakyas, I lived in the depths of the palace, guarded by high fortress walls and an army of soldiers. Yet even though I was surrounded by ranks of well-trained palace guards, I never knew a moment's peace of mind or freedom from the suspicion that an enemy might somehow manage to attack. But now that I live alone in the forest, wearing the coarse robes of a monk and devoting myself to meditation in the hope of enlightenment, those fears and suspicions have vanished without a trace. At first I feared that the life of a monk would be a painful one, that I would lose all sense of freedom through being bound by the precepts. But as, in accordance with the holy teachings, I tried to cast aside my former self and persevered in the practices of meditation and of begging for my daily food, the life that I had thought would be so painful came to seem sweet. Last night, as I meditated, I felt as if something that had been binding me body and soul had suddenly snapped. I was overcome with a sense of inexpressible joy and freedom. I must have uttered the words 'Ah, how pleasant! What a wonderful feeling!' unconsciously. I don't actually remember saying anything."

The Buddha nodded slowly as he listened, as if with satisfaction. Bhaddiya continued: "In the palace I ate the rarest delicacies, wore clothes of fine silk, and was served by many slaves and attendants. Night after night I gave myself up to pleasure, yet remained somehow unsatisfied. I've found true happiness only now that I've left the palace behind, exchanged golden plates for a mendicant's iron bowl and gorgeous robes for a monk's coarse garments, and learned to move from place to place begging for my daily food. That's why I must have cried out with joy during the meditation session."

When he finished speaking, the other monks exclaimed in amazement, and the Buddha praised him, saying, "Bhaddiya, you have done well in attaining the state of fearlessness, the state of true spiritual peace. You are first among those who have left behind the worldly honors to which they were born and have succeeded in achieving true nobility—the nobility of the spirit."

Encouraged by these words, Bhaddiya embarked with renewed determination upon the Pure Practices, which would ultimately lead him to the state of an *arahant,* one free of all worldly defilements.

TISSA
The Old Man Who Loved Leisure

Old, fat Tissa," as he was called, was Shakya-muni's cousin. He was the son of Amita, who was the sister of King Suddhodana, Shakyamuni's father. Tissa entered the Sangha at quite an advanced age. By that time the Buddha's fame had spread far and wide, and the cream of Shakya youth had already entered the religious life.

Tissa did not want to be left behind, so he too set off for the Jetavana Monastery, where the Buddha was staying. He asked for and was granted admission to the Sangha, but soon he began to complain about the severity of the monastic life. It was almost unbearably hard for Tissa, who was accustomed to a life of luxury, to have to stand in front of people's gates early in the morning, begging his daily food, or to have to sit for long hours in meditation outdoors.

He thought, "There's no point in my trying to follow these practices designed for youngsters—not at my age. I've lived a long time and learned a lot in my years at court. I'm sure I can find my own road to enlightenment." Thus Tissa persuaded himself to abandon the various practices that Buddhist monks are supposed to observe. He began to wear soft robes of fine cloth and to spend his days sitting idly in the main hall of the monastery, hardly troubling to move his corpulent form. Taking advantage of his fellow monks' reserved silence toward him, he set about living the life of a retired gentleman in the midst of their monastic exertions.

One day a group of monks came from a distant monastery to see the Buddha. Arriving at the Jetavana Monastery, the travelers saw Tissa planted in the middle of the main hall and thought he must be a senior monk of great distinction. They approached and bowed deeply, and one addressed him: "Reverend sir, we have traveled far, hoping to see the Buddha. Would you be good enough to take us to him?"

Tissa just stared at the monk, not deigning to respond. Again the monk spoke to him respectfully, but he maintained his stony silence. The monk spoke a third time, a look of puzzlement on his face: "Forgive me, but have you been practicing the monastic life for a very long time?"

When he heard this question, Tissa's face darkened. He assumed the other was judging him to be a monk advanced in years but poor in practice, and his proud, stubborn spirit was outraged at the very suggestion. "How long have I been a monk? Not long—only a few months. So what?" he retorted.

Taken aback by these angry words, the monk ventured to reproach Tissa for his arrogant attitude: "Friend, you are mature in years, yet I can't help feeling sorry for you. Not only did you fail to respond to our greetings, but you seem to be completely unaware of your own arrogance and rudeness."

Tissa became even more agitated. "Just who do you

think you are, you young puppy of a monk!" he shouted. "Do you have any idea whom you are addressing? I am of noble Shakya blood, just like the Buddha himself; and I have more in the way of knowledge and experience than you young fools will gain in a lifetime. I'll show you a thing or two—just you follow me!" His face red with anger, Tissa stretched out trembling hands and heaved his fat body to a standing position; then he marched the visitors off to meet the Buddha, rather as if they were prisoners and he their jailer.

"These monks who've just come to the monastery have been abusing and reviling me for no reason at all. How can anyone be so rude and unfeeling?" Tissa complained when they were in the presence of the Buddha. Tissa's lips trembled as he spoke, and his eyes were red and bleary with barely suppressed tears.

The Buddha gazed calmly at Tissa and spoke: "Tissa, when these wandering monks arrived at our monastery, did you rise and greet them? Did you make them welcome after their long journey?"

Tissa was at a loss for words; all he could do was shake his head in reply.

"Did you offer them something to slake their thirst? Did you give them water with which to wash the dust from their feet?"

"No," said Tissa quietly, again shaking his head.

"Did you prepare rooms for them to stay in?"

He could only shake his head yet again.

"Well, then, Tissa, wouldn't it be fair to say that you failed to carry out any of your duties as a senior monk? You say you were subjected to abuse and contempt for no reason; but would it not be truer to say that your own attitude was the cause of the ill treatment you complain of? Tissa, always remember that no matter how others treat you, as a monk your duty is to endure it with patience and use it as an opportunity for self-reflection. That is how a truly noble person must react. Tissa, your great work now must be to learn to control your pride and anger. That is your path to enlightenment."

Abashed, Tissa resolved to begin his religious life over again and follow the precepts exactly this time, devoting himself to serious religious practice. Eventually he set out on a pilgrimage, walking from town to town and village to village as a mendicant. It was a truly hard exercise for Tissa, old and fat as he was.

By the time Tissa reached the monastery outside the village of Kitagiri in the kingdom of Kasi, he had lost all energy and will to continue his pilgrimage. Moreover, as his stay at the Kitagiri monastery stretched on, he began to forget the Buddha's admonition. He neglected even the customary morning begging round and relied on offerings brought to the monastery by pious lay believers. He had fallen again into an idle pattern of life. At this time there were at the monastery four other monks who had grown weary of the life of pilgrimage and mendicancy, and they joined Tissa in his indolent ways, forming a kind of "do-nothing brotherhood."

One day news came that the Buddha, accompanied by a great number of disciples, was approaching Kitagiri. "The Buddha's coming!" cried the five indolent monks, suddenly galvanized into action. They began feverishly to clean the little monastery inside and out. Suddenly one of them said, "If all those monks are planning to spend the night here, we'll find ourselves sleeping outside, my friends." They decided to divide the bedding and dishes among themselves, putting some aside only for the Buddha. These articles were, of course, intended for the common use of all members of the Sangha.

Soon the Buddha arrived at the monastery, accompanied by Sariputta, Moggallana, and many other disciples. The five monks greeted the party respectfully and escorted the Buddha to the quarters they had prepared for him. "You must be tired after your long journey," one of them said. "We have made ready your room, your bedding, and your dishes, in expectation of your arrival. Please rest and recover from the rigors of your pilgrimage."

"Thank you very much," replied the Buddha. "Would you also please prepare rooms and bedding for my companions?"

To this the monk falteringly replied, "We have been busy preaching the Dharma in this region, using this little monastery as our base. As you can see, it's a small, poor place. We don't have any spare rooms or bedding to accommodate so many visitors. We're terribly sorry, but we'll have to ask the reverend monks to take their rest outside, under the trees."

The Buddha responded to the monk's feeble excuse in a resounding voice: "Listen to what I have to say! There are five acts that are intolerable in the religious life; these five are equivalent to theft and are called the Five Robbers. The first is to neglect to observe the precepts and at the same time conspire with one's fellow monks to squander the offerings made by the faithful for the support of worthy monks. The second is to harbor evil thoughts and do impure deeds and at the same time pretend to be a decent, worthy monk in front of others. The third is to grow arrogant because of one's knowledge and look with contempt on other monks. The fourth is to think nothing of trampling on the rights and dignity of others in order to ensure food and clothing for oneself. The fifth is to treat the common possessions of the Sangha as if they were one's own. Let no one who treads the holy path to enlightenment even think of doing such deeds!"

Each of these words stabbed Tissa's conscience like a knife. Throwing himself down before the Buddha, he confessed his wrongdoing and vowed to renew his religious practice. He thought, "This time I must practice according to the Buddha's instructions. If I cannot attain enlightenment even then, I will cast aside this worthless life of mine without regret."

Having made this great resolution, Tissa returned to the Jetavana Monastery and threw himself into both meditation and mendicancy. He worked very hard, observing all the Buddha's precepts and instructions to the letter. When, as a result of earnest practice, he was able to master a particular point of the Buddha's teachings, a feeling of cool refreshment seemed to pervade his body and mind.

Unfortunately, feelings of pride and self-satisfaction began to arise again when he had completed a certain amount of religious practice. He wondered if that was all there was to the Dharma. He felt that he had already mastered the Buddha's teachings. Then— perhaps because age had made him physically and mentally weary—his feeling of pride was replaced by a bleak sense of emptiness. He expressed his feeling of futility to his fellow monks: "Friends, I've devoted myself sincerely to religious practice, but now it all seems pointless. I'm tired. This Dharma that everyone talks about isn't such a great thing after all. Following the Way and all that is meaningless."

The other monks, fearing for his sanity, went and told the Buddha about his recent comments. The Buddha immediately summoned Tissa.

"Tissa, I have some questions to ask you. Various phenomena arise in this world. If we allow ourselves to become attached to these phenomena, can we evade suffering and sorrow when the phenomena change or disappear, as they must?"

Tissa replied, "It is impossible to evade sorrow and suffering as long as we remain attached to phenomena, which arise and disappear moment by moment."

The Buddha nodded. "An excellent reply, Tissa. Well, then, if we are attached to our own feelings and views, will we experience pain and sorrow when circumstances force changes in those feelings and views?"

"Sorrow and pain are inevitable as long as we remain attached to our own feelings and views."

"Tissa, how well you understand the nature of things. Well, then, is there anything in this world that never changes?"

"Not one of the myriad phenomena that arise in this world is unchanging."

The Buddha nodded again and addressed the following words to Tissa, speaking very slowly and carefully: "Tissa, you understand the nature of reality clearly. You know that one can never be free from pain and sorrow as long as one is attached to phenomena in this impermanent world. How, then, is one to sever the bonds of attachment?

"Let me tell you a story. Once upon a time a man who had lost his way asked one who knew the road how he should proceed. The one who knew the road answered, 'You must go straight ahead for some time.

The road divides into two farther on. Disregard the left-hand path and keep to the right. A little farther on you will come to a great, dark forest. Do not be concerned; just keep straight on. After a bit you will find yourself at the edge of a deep marsh; again, keep going. Next you will encounter a steep, craggy mountain. Do not be disturbed, though; go straight along the path, and eventually you will reach a broad, level plain, which is your destination.'

"Tissa, the man who has lost his way represents the ordinary, unenlightened mortal. The one who knows the road is the Buddha. The division in the path represents doubts along the way, and the correct path to the right is the Eightfold Path. The dark forest symbolizes illusion; the great marsh, greed; the steep mountains, anger, suffering, and sorrow. The broad plain that lies beyond all these obstacles is nirvana, the realm of absolute peace.

"Tissa, there is no need for you to be troubled in mind. Just follow to the end the path I have shown you. At the end of it, you will find the realm of absolute peace, I promise you."

It was as if the dark clouds of doubt and despair surrounding Tissa's heart had been pierced by a ray of brilliant light. From that moment "the mind that seeks the Way without turning back" took firm root within him.

The *Theragatha* contains the following passage ascribed to Tissa: "Just as one pulls out the sword stuck in his body or hurries to extinguish the fire set on the turban he is wearing, so the monk should go on pilgrimage with care."

PUNNA
The Man of Courage

The wealthy merchant Punna, taken to see Shakyamuni at the Jetavana Monastery by Sudatta,
who had donated the monastery to the Sangha, immediately requested permission to become a disciple.
Shakyamuni said to him, "Punna, I hear that you live
in a distant land to the west. It was good of you to
come so far. Now devote yourself to following the path
to enlightenment. I hear too that you are a wealthy
merchant. What made you decide to give up secular
life for the life of religion?"

Punna thereupon told Shakyamuni his story. Born
in the town of Supparaka, in the land of Sunaparanta
on the west coast of India, he was the son of a merchant. He and his brothers were on bad terms, and
ultimately they drove him out of the house. But Punna
had inherited his father's talent for business. He was
so well spoken and reliable that the business he started
for himself prospered and grew.

From a firewood merchant he purchased a quantity
of precious aromatic wood called oxhead sandalwood.
Making a perilous sea voyage, he sold the wood in
other countries at an immense profit and returned

safely home. Soon his name was known in all the cities of India, including Savatthi, the capital of Kosala, where a group of merchants decided to visit him to ask if they could accompany him on his next voyage. Since they had come all the way from Savatthi, Punna felt he could not refuse their request. Taking them with him, he put out to sea once again.

They had not been at sea long when Punna noticed that the merchants gathered together and recited something every morning and evening. He finally asked what they were singing, and one of them replied, "We are not singing; we are chanting words taught us by Shakyamuni."

Not knowing who Shakyamuni was, Punna asked about him and was told, "He was born a prince of the Shakya tribe but gave up the secular life to become the most revered teacher in the world. He trained himself in the mountains and forests and ultimately attained supreme enlightenment. Because of his great virtue he is called Shakyamuni, the Sage of the Shakyas."

As they talked of Shakyamuni, Punna was deeply moved and made up his mind to go hear him teach the moment the journey ended. When he asked where Shakyamuni could be found, one of the merchants said, "At the Jetavana Monastery, which Sudatta built for him outside Savatthi."

As soon as Punna returned home, he went to his oldest brother to say he wanted to give up secular life for the life of religion. His brother expressed shock that, having grown so rich, Punna could be dissatisfied with his way of life. "With all your money, you can select a bride from among the very best families. Why don't you think about settling down and marrying?"

But seeing that Punna was determined, his brother had no choice but to give his consent.

Punna told this story to Shakyamuni and concluded by saying, "I was introduced to Sudatta by the Savatthi merchants, and Sudatta brought me here. I now respectfully ask to be allowed to join the Sangha."

After praising Punna's determination to pursue the Way to enlightenment, Shakyamuni turned to Sudatta and said, "You have brought me a priceless gem." Shakyamuni immediately began showing Punna the Way by teaching him about liberation from attachments resulting from the so-called six entrances: the eyes, ears, nose, tongue, body, and mind.

Following a period of training and discipline with the Buddha, one day Punna said to him, "Revered teacher, I would like to bring happiness to the people of my land, Sunaparanta, by carrying your teachings to them. May I have your permission to do so?"

No one in that far land had heard the Buddha's teachings. Knowing how difficult it would be to introduce them, Shakyamuni tested Punna's resolve by asking him, "Punna, the people of Sunaparanta are supposed to be rough and villainous. What will you do if they despise, ridicule, and revile you?"

Punna replied. "Revered teacher, I will think that they are good people for not beating or stoning me."

"And what," continued Shakyamuni, "will you do if they throw stones at you or beat you with sticks?"

"I will think they are good people for not injuring me with knives," Punna answered.

"And suppose they kill you?"

"Revered teacher, I have heard that one of your disciples once killed himself with a sword because he was repelled by his own body, which was prisoner to the five desires—to enjoy beautiful sights, pleasant sounds, pleasant odors, good food, and the touch of pleasant things. If they take my life, I will revere the people of Sunaparanta for their supreme mercy in liberating me from a body controlled by the five desires."

Seeing that Punna would be able to handle even the most difficult situation, Shakyamuni said, "You have spoken well, Punna. You have disciplined yourself in the Way and have learned forbearance. With your firm resolve to find enlightenment, you will certainly be able to teach and guide the people of Sunaparanta. Go and teach those people, who do not know mental tranquillity yet. Expound the Dharma to them and bring them true peace."

Punna's innate abilities enabled him to develop extraordinary eloquence and thus to be counted among the Buddha's most important disciples. His determination to carry the teachings of Shakyamuni to all people, no matter where they lived, further refined his talents. He deeply believed that to teach others it was essential to revere the buddha-nature within them, their inherent potential for enlightenment, even if they intended harm.

On reaching Sunaparanta, Punna found lodging outside Supparaka. The following morning, as he was about to enter the town to beg for food, he encountered a hunter with bow in hand. Punna had a sudden premonition of evil and cautioned him against going hunting that day. Enraged that a passing monk should make such an ill-omened remark to him, the hunter put arrow to bow and aimed at Punna. Without flinching, Punna opened his robe and cried, "If you are going to shoot, shoot me here, in the belly!"

The hunter was taken aback by Punna's composure. Still with his abdomen uncovered, Punna advanced toward him and said, "For the sake of food, human beings set traps for the birds of the air and slay the deer of the forests. Among themselves, they battle with swords, slaughtering one another. Some people are so hungry that they swallow balls of iron to assuage the pangs. I myself have been unable to break free of the suffering caused by the desire to preserve life by satisfying my belly. Shoot me there."

It is said that, overwhelmed by such courage, the hunter begged forgiveness of Punna, who then began patiently to explain the Dharma and converted him to faith in the teachings of Shakyamuni. Through his willingness to go to any length, even to the point of laying down his own life, Punna led five hundred people in Sunaparanta to Buddhism.

GLOSSARY

Where the transliteration of Pali or Sanskrit words used in the text differs from the orthodox form, the latter is given in parentheses with correct diacritical markings. In the abbreviations used here, P stands for Pali and S for Sanskrit.

Ambapali (Ambapālī, P; Āmrapālī, S)   A courtesan who became a disciple of the Buddha.

Ananda (Ānanda, P, S)   A cousin of Shakyamuni and one of the ten great disciples of the Buddha. One of the six young Shakya nobles who became disciples of the Buddha. He was foremost in hearing many teachings.

Anga (Aṅga, P, S)   One of the sixteen major kingdoms of India in Shakyamuni's time.

Anupiya (Anupiyā, P; Anupriya, S)   The town in Malla where the Buddha received the six young Shakya nobles into the Sangha.

Anuruddha (P; Aniruddha, S)   A cousin of Shakyamuni, and one of the ten great disciples of the Buddha. One of the six young Shakya nobles who became disciples of the Buddha. He was foremost in divine insight.

arahant (P; *arhat,* S)   Literally, "person of worth, honorable one." A person who is free from all cravings and thus from rebirth.

Asita (P, S)   An uncle of Kacchayana, and a hermit-seer who prophesied that if Shakyamuni remained in the secular world he would become a "wheel-rolling king" and that if he abandoned the secular world for the life of religion he would become a buddha.

Avanti (P, S) One of the sixteen major kingdoms of India in Shakyamuni's time.

Bamboo Grove Monastery (Veḷuvanārāma, P; Veṇuvanārāma, S) The first monastery of the Sangha, built by King Bimbisara outside Rajagaha.

Bhadda (Bhaddā, P; Bhadrā, S) A rich man's daughter who married the robber chieftain Satthuka and later became a disciple of the Buddha.

Bhaddiya (P; Bhadrika or Bhadraka, S) The king of the Shakyas after the death of King Suddhodhana, and one of the six young Shakya nobles who became disciples of the Buddha. He was a cousin of Anuruddha.

Bhagu (P; Bhṛgu, S) One of the six young Shakya nobles who became disciples of the Buddha.

Bimbisara (Bimbisāra, P, S) The king of Magadha, and a lay disciple of the Buddha.

bodhi (P, S) Wisdom, enlightenment, buddhahood.

Brahman (*brāhmaṇa*, P, S) The priestly caste, highest of the four major castes of India.

buddha (P, S) A title meaning "one who is enlightened" or "enlightened one."

Champa (Campā, P, S) The capital of Anga.

Channa (P; Chanda or Chandaka, S) A slave who served at the royal court of Kapilavatthu and later became a disciple of the Buddha.

Chitta-Hatthisariputta (Citta-Hatthisāriputta, P; Citra-Hastiroha-putra, S) A farmer who became a disciple of the Buddha.

Chunda (Cunda, P, S) A blacksmith who was a lay disciple of the Buddha. He prepared the meal that led to the Buddha's final illness.

Dabba-Mallaputta (P; Darva-Mallaputra, S) A senior monk who voluntarily undertook to perform services for the other members of the Sangha.

Deer Park (Migadāya, P; Mṛgadāva, S) A park near Varanasi where Shakyamuni preached his first sermon, shortly after his enlightenment.

Devadatta (P, S) Ananda's older brother, and one of the six young Shakya nobles who became disciples of the Buddha. He attempted to disrupt the Sangha and on many occasions tried to harm the Buddha.

Dhammadinna (Dhammadinnā, P; Dharmadinnā, S)   A rich man's wife who became a disciple of the Buddha. She was foremost among nuns in preaching.

Dhammapada (P)   "Verses on the Law." One of the oldest extant Buddhist scriptures.

Dharma (S; Dhamma, P)   1. The universal norms or laws that govern human existence; commonly translated as "Law" or "Truth." 2. The teachings of the Buddha.

Eightfold Path   Right view, right thinking, right speech, right action, right livelihood, right endeavor, right mindfulness, right meditation.

First Council   The first assembly of Buddhist monks, which met some three months after the Buddha's death to collect the Buddha's teachings.

five precepts   The basic precepts of the lay Buddhist: not to take life, not to steal, not to indulge in sexual misconduct, not to lie, and not to drink intoxicants.

five supernatural powers   Highly sensitive faculties enabling one to see things ordinary people cannot see, hear things they cannot hear, read their minds, know their pasts, and act with perfect freedom.

Four Noble Truths   1. All existence entails suffering: the Truth of Suffering. 2. Suffering is caused by ignorance, which gives rise to craving and illusion: the Truth of Cause. 3. There is an end to suffering, and this state of no suffering is called nirvana: the Truth of Extinction. 4. Nirvana is attained through the practice of the Eightfold Path: the Truth of the Path. The Four Noble Truths, one of the most fundamental Buddhist teachings, was the subject of the Buddha's first sermon.

Gabled Hall (Kūṭāgārasālā, P; Kūṭāgāraśālā, S)   A monastery in a forest on the outskirts of Vesali.

Gaya (Gayā, P, S)   The place where Shakyamuni attained enlightenment, in Magadha.

Ghosita Monastery (Ghositārāma, P, S)   A monastery in Kosambi.

Isidasi (Isidāsī, P; Ṛṣidāsī, S)   A member of the Shakya tribe, and the daughter of a rich merchant in Ujjeni. She became a disciple of the Buddha.

Jetavana Monastery (Jetārāma, P, S) A monastery on the southern outskirts of Savatthi, built on land donated by Sudatta.

Kacchayana (Kaccāyana, P; Kātyāyana, S) One of the ten great disciples of the Buddha. He was foremost in explaining the Dharma.

Kapilavatthu (P; Kapilavastu, S) The capital of the Shakya state.

Kasi (Kāsi, P; Kāśi, S) One of the sixteen major kingdoms of India in Shakyamuni's time.

Kimbila (P, S) One of the six young Shakya nobles who became disciples of the Buddha.

Kondanna (Koṇḍañña, P; Kauṇḍinya, S) A senior monk, and the uncle of Punna-Mantaniputta.

Kosala (P, S) The most powerful of the sixteen major kingdoms of India in Shakyamuni's time.

Kosambi (Kosambī, P; Kauśāmbī, S) The capital of Vamsa, and a prosperous trade center.

Kshatriya (kṣatriya, S; khattiya, P) The warrior caste, second highest of the four major castes of India.

Kuru (P, S) A tribal kingdom northwest of Kosala.

Kusinara (Kusinārā, P; Kuśinagara, S) The capital of Malla, and the place where the Buddha died.

Kutadanta (Kūṭadanta, P, S) A Brahman who became a lay disciple of the Buddha.

Magadha (P, S) One of the sixteen major kingdoms of India in Shakyamuni's time.

Maha-Kassapa (Mahā-Kassapa, P; Mahā-Kāśyapa, S) One of the ten great disciples of the Buddha. He was foremost in ascetic practices.

Mahapajapati (Mahāpajāpatī, P; Mahāprajāpatī, S) The younger sister of Maya, who married Suddhodana after Maya's death and reared Shakyamuni. The mother of Nanda and Sundarinanda, she became the first Buddhist nun.

Malla (P, S) One of the sixteen major kingdoms of India in Shakyamuni's time.

Maya (Māyā, P, S) The mother of Shakyamuni.

Migaramata Hall (Migāramātu-pāsāda, P; Mṛgāramātṛ-prāsāda, S) A monastery built by the female lay disciple Visakha in a park on the eastern outskirts of Savatthi. Migaramata (Migāramātar, P; Mṛgāramātṛ, S), "Mother of Migara," was an honorific title of Visakha.

Moggallana (Moggallāna, P; Maudgalyāyana, S)   One of the ten great disciples of the Buddha. He was foremost in supernatural powers.

Nanda (P, S)   The older brother of Sundarinanda and the younger half brother of Shakyamuni. He became a disciple of the Buddha.

Nigantha-Nataputta (Nigaṇṭha-Nātaputta, P; Nirgrantha-Jñātaputra, S)   The founder of the Jain faith, and one of the six non-Buddhist teachers.

Nigrodha Monastery (Nigrodhārāma, P; Nyagrodhārāma, S)   A monastery outside Kapilavatthu.

nirvana (*nirvāṇa*, S; *nibbāna*, P)   Literally, "extinction." 1. The state of enlightenment attained by the Buddha. 2. The highest state of enlightenment. 3. Emancipation from all forms of existence.

Pajjota (P; Pradyota, S)   The king of Avanti.

Pasenadi (P; Prasenajit, S)   The king of Kosala, and a lay disciple of the Buddha.

Pataliputta (Pāṭaliputta, P; Pāṭaliputra, S)   A city in northern Magadha; present-day Patna.

Pava (Pāvā, P, S)   The village in Malla where the Buddha ate the meal that led to his final illness.

Punna (Puṇṇa, P; Pūrṇa, S)   A wealthy merchant from Sunaparanta who became a disciple of the Buddha.

Punna (Puṇṇā, P; Pūrṇā, S)   The maid of Sujata, and a lay disciple of the Buddha.

Punna-Mantaniputta (Puṇṇa-Mantāniputta, P; Pūrṇa-Maitrāyanīputra, S)   One of the ten great disciples of the Buddha. He was foremost in teaching the Dharma.

Rahula (Rāhula, P, S)   The only son of Shakyamuni, born before Shakyamuni's renunciation of the world, and one of the ten great disciples of the Buddha. He was foremost in quietly doing good.

Rajagaha (Rājagaha, P; Rājagṛha, S)   The capital of Magadha; present-day Rajgir.

Saketa (Sāketa, P; Śāketa, S)   A city in Kosala.

Sangha (*saṅgha*, P, S)   The monastic community of Buddhist monks or nuns; more generally, the community of Buddhist believers.

Sanjaya (Sañjaya, P, S)   A skeptic, and one of the six non-Buddhist teachers.

Sariputta (Sāriputta, P; Śāriputra, S)   One of the ten great disciples of the Buddha. He was foremost in wisdom.

Savatthi (Sāvatthī, P; Śrāvastī, S)   The capital of Kosala.

Shakya (Śākya, S; Sakya, P)   The tribe to which Shakyamuni belonged.

Shakyamuni (Śākyamuni, S; Sakyamuni, P)   Literally, "Sage of the Shakyas"; a title of the Buddha.

Siddhattha (P; Siddhārtha, S)   Literally, "he who has accomplished his aim"; the personal name of the Buddha before his renunciation of the world.

Siha (Sīha, P; Siṃha, S)   A general who converted from the Jain faith to Buddhism.

Siha (Sīhā, P; Siṃhā, S)   A niece of General Siha who became a disciple of the Buddha.

Sona (Soṇā, P; Śroṇā, S)   The daughter of a rich merchant in Savatthi, and a disciple of the Buddha. She was foremost in practice among nuns.

Subhuti (Subhūti, P, S)   One of the ten great disciples of the Buddha. He was foremost in understanding the doctrine of the Void.

Sudatta (P, S)   A wealthy merchant of Savatthi, and a lay disciple of the Buddha. He donated the land on which the Jetavana Monastery was built.

Suddhodana (P; Śuddhodana, S)   The king of the Shakyas, and the father of Shakyamuni.

Sudra (śūdra, S; sudda, P)   The lowest of the four major castes of India.

Sujata (Sujātā, P, S)   The young woman who gave Shakyamuni a bowl of milk gruel before his attainment of enlightenment. She became the first female lay disciple of the Buddha.

Sunaparanta (Sunāparanta, P; Sunāparantaka, S)   A country on the west coast of India.

Sundarinanda (Sundarīnandā, P, S)   The younger sister of Nanda and the younger half sister of Shakyamuni. She became a disciple of the Buddha.

Sunita (Sunīta, P, S)   A Sudra who became a disciple of the Buddha.

Theragatha (*Theragāthā*, P)   "Verses of the Elder Monks." A collection of verses attributed to monks who were disciples of the Buddha.

Therigatha (*Therīgāthā*, P)   "Verses of the Elder Nuns." A collection of verses attributed to nuns who were disciples of the Buddha.

Three Treasures   The Buddha, the Dharma, and the Sangha.

Tissa (P; Tiṣya, S)   A cousin of Shakyamuni who became a disciple at an advanced age.

Ugga (P; Ugra, S)   A householder of Vesali who became a lay disciple of the Buddha.

Ujjeni (Ujjenī, P; Ujjāyinī, S)   The capital of Avanti, and the birthplace of Kacchayana.

Upali (Upāli, P, S)   A barber who became one of the ten great disciples of the Buddha. He was foremost in keeping the precepts.

Uruvela (Uruvelā, P; Uruvilvā, S)   A village near Gaya.

Vaishya (vaiśya, S; vessa, P)   The merchant caste, third of the four major castes of India.

Vajji (Vajjī, P; Vṛji, S)   A tribal confederation, one of the sixteen major kingdoms of India in Shakyamuni's time.

Vamsa (Vaṃsā, P; Vatsā, S)   One of the sixteen major kingdoms of India in Shakyamuni's time.

Varanasi (Vārāṇasī, P, S)   A city on the Ganges in Kasi.

Vedas (veda, P, S)   The basic Brahmanic scriptures, composed between 2000 and 500 B.C. They consist of the Rig-veda, Sama-veda, Yajur-veda, and Atharva-veda.

Vesali (Vesāli, P; Vaiśali, S)   The capital of the Vajji confederation.

Visakha (Visākha, P; Viśākha, S)   A rich man of Rajagaha, and the husband of Dhammadinna.

Visakha (Visākhā, P; Viśākhā, S)   A rich man's daughter who became a lay disciple of the Buddha. She was foremost among women in giving.

Vulture Peak (Gijjhakūṭa, P; Gṛdhrakūṭa, S)   A mountain near Rajagaha, so named because of the shape of its peak and because many vultures are supposed to have lived on the mountain.

wheel-rolling king (cakkavatti-rāja, P; cakravarti-rāja, S)   In Indian mythology, an ideal ruler.

World-honored One (bhagavat, P, S)   An epithet of a buddha.

Yasodhara (Yasodharā, P; Yaśodharā, S)   The wife of Shakyamuni before he renounced the world, and the mother of Rahula. She became a disciple of the Buddha.